Obedience Training for Recorders

a care and maintenance manual

Tim Cranmore

First published in May 2009 by

Peacock Press
Scout Bottom Farm
Mytholmroyd
Hebden Bridge HX7 5JS

ISBN: 978-1-904846-37-6

British Library Cataloguing in Publication Data

A record is available from the British Library

Copyright © Tim Cranmore 2009

All rights reserved. No part of this publication may be reproduced, stored in a retrieval system, transmitted in any form or by any means electronic, mechanical, including photocopying, recording or otherwise without prior consent of the copyright holders.

Designed by D&P Design and Print
Printed by Lightning Source UK

Contents

CHAPTER 1	Where it all started	1
CHAPTER 2	Basic Training	7
CHAPTER 3	Advanced Training	21
CHAPTER 4	Really Major Surgery [WARNING – could be fatal!]	35
CHAPTER 5	Tuning with the Bore and Fingerholes	43
CHAPTER 6	Miscellaneous	57
	Appendix – a list of current active recorder makers	61

CHAPTER 1

Where it all started

It is a mystery to many how the English settled on the word recorder to describe a new musical instrument that had arrived from Europe together with the renaissance. In Italy, probably the home of the instrument, they described it as 'flauto dolce', sweet flute, romantic and true to the sound, While passing through France the locals christened it 'la *flûte à bec*', the flute with the beak, visually descriptive, in Germany it became ' die Blockflöte', *the flute with a block*, functional and Teutonic, yet in England, someone picked up one of these new instruments and called it a recorder!

Historically, the word first appears in English in the accounts of the Earl of Derby [later Henry IV] in 1388 – was it his idea? Why? 600 odd years later, and in a digital age, did they not foresee the difficulties which that would give rise to?

Look on Google; '*flûte à bec*' gives 359,000 hits [correct at 19/3/09], 'Blockflöte', 397,000, 'flauto dolce', 549,000, [O those verbose Italians], but 'recorder', a massive 64,200,000!!. Does this mean that we love the recorder to bits? – no, it means that we are competing in our definition with digital recorders, video recorders, cockpit voice recorders, the Douglas County Recorder P.O. Box 218 Minden, Nevada and so on and so forth, for the attention of the world. Pity the poor web designer given the job of getting a recorder site to the first search page.

Now, dear reader, assuming that you are one of the fortunate few who have waded through 64 million references and found the real thing, you will find yourself in charge of a new pet, one that can purr like a well fed pussycat, or an uncontrollable and unpredictable beast that spits [literally] and growls like a one-eyed feral dingo. This book, like the late Barbara Woodhouse, will show you how to take your recorder for walkies in respectable musical society, and still stand proud!

I ought to add that several recorders have passed through my workshop having either been chewed, or indeed totally destroyed, by various breeds of dog. Cats flee from them, geckos may use them as a perch while waiting for a passing fly, but only our canine friends feel such affinity with the recorder that they relish it for lunch!

The Recorder – how it works – basically.

A recorder is actually a very cleverly constructed and interconnected series of holes, which are occupied by a small section of the atmosphere, which is technically connected by means of this to every point on the planet, but not beyond. As you energise that column of air it vibrates giving out the sounds that we hear as music, and this sound travels out – in theory – to every point on the surface of the earth, however faintly. However, we have to compete with birds, bees and Radio1, so your parents and friends generally cannot hear you practising in the garden shed, which was probably the whole point of sending you there

Obedience Training for Recorders - *Tim Cranmore*

in the first place! [It could probably also in theory be picked up by extraterrestrials by pointing a very sensitive vibration detector at the upper atmosphere, but as they wouldn't know what they were looking for in the first place the chances of them using the recorder as a justification for the destruction of planet Earth are slim].

Counting the number of outside holes in a normal treble recorder gives a grand total of 14, each of which is designed to do a particular job. Starting at the top, the windway entrance acts as the air intake, energy from the muscles in your diaphragm forces air into the windway, which shapes it and accelerates it towards the windway exit.

Leaving the windway as a laminar flow, and carefully directed by the chamfers on the block and the windway roof, the air crosses a gap of approx 4.5mm. in a treble recorder and hits the labium, a sharp edge carved into the wood [or plastic] – here it vacillates like a floating voter – up or down – above or below – and as it does so it generates the vibration which is expressed as sound, and is transmitted to the air column of the recorder.

The length of a recorder tube is, of course, defined by which fingerholes are open. The more that are open, the shorter the tube, the higher the note, and if you give it a bit of a kick, or open up the thumbhole a fraction, the air column flips to the next harmonic and so on, giving a potential range of two and a half octaves for a baroque recorder.

In a medieval recorder with a parallel bore, an octave and a half is all there is to it, however, coupled with the desire during the renaissance to improve everything from drains to weapons of mass destruction, the shape of the column of air, otherwise known as the bore profile, was refined in order to extend the range, simplify the fingering, and enable bigger and better tubes with keys, fontanelles and other fancy bits, and the very distinctive recorder sound that we know today began to evolve.

The Recorder - a brief history

A recorder is a resonator – and Homo Sapiens has been using resonators since it first learnt to swing a stick at a mammoth rib cage and accidentally invented the xylophone. Seriously though, bone flutes turn up all over the world from about 8 thousand years ago; the flute and other wind instruments featured heavily in the bible [as Jericho found to its cost,] and more concrete evidence comes from many ancient civilisations to show that we have been happily fluting and tooting away since our cultural infancy. However, the recorder as we know it begins to figure in European art and in excavations from the 14th century.

Medieval musicians [14th-15th cent] obviously suffered from severe constipation, as they often took their recorders with them to pass the time when they 'went'. This conclusion is based on the fact that most surviving medieval recorders were found during the excavation of long drop latrines. Conversely, one could argue that picking up one's recorder from the floor was an easier task than fishing it out of the loo, which is why medieval recorders were often abandoned in such circumstances! Another was found in a millrace, and another in the foundations of a house, but none were lovingly preserved as a cultural artefact.

These instruments vary greatly in design, they were all small, but they were all well made. This was not an unsophisticated peasant instrument, but a professional tool.

Renaissance musicians [15th-17th cent] entered a more developed cultural landscape, where much was expected of both composers and performers, and consequently of instrument makers.

All aspects of artistic, social and political life were re-examined and refined to suit the tastes of the European court and church, and the recorder was no exception. In England, Henry VIII actually imported his very own family of Italian instrument makers, the Bassanos, to make sure that he was at the cutting edge of good taste, and an inventory of his instruments at his death includes a collection of more than 70 recorders.

We have many surviving recorders from this time in museum collections around the world, especially Vienna and Nuremburg, which vary in size from tiny ivory flageolets and sopraninos, to the extended great bass in Antwerp with a speaking length of 2.4 metres. Now in the cultural mainstream, the recorder was transformed into a consort instrument, a bit like an organ with fingerholes, and took its place alongside brass [cornetti and sacbuts], and strings [viols] in the multichoir music of the Italian courts and churches.

Whether it was also used as a solo instrument in respectable circles is debatable. Nowadays, reams of solo music from the period is played in recorder editions for recorder players, but the existence of actual solo recorders and designated solo repertoire is open to argument, and such music was more likely to have been played on violins or cornetti. A notable exception in Holland was Jacob van Eyck whose published variations on popular hymns and folk songs are specifically given as recorder music.

Baroque musicians were presented with a shift in emphasis from the group to the soloist. With florid arias, rattling concertos, organ fireworks, professional musicians left the churches and courts and became showmen.

The great makers of the age such as Bressan, Stanesby and Denner, were able to build on more than 400 years of experience to produce outstanding instruments, some of which have been preserved in museum collections. But in terms of speed, agility, dynamic range and emotional depth, the recorder was rather left behind as the Baroque era developed, and became the instrument of the sound effect, allegory, and the noble amateur, whose accomplishments had, by definition, to include musical skills as well as art, horsemanship, swordplay and charming the ladies of the court. Serious music was still written for the recorder by serious composers such as Handel and Telemann, but also there was a lot of drivel – endless duets in parallel thirds, short on both length and content.

The baroque flute, louder and more flexible, took the place of the recorder in the orchestral soundscape, and the recorder appeared to fade, or at least in popular myth it did, but in fact the recorder took on a whole new life. Becoming shorter and shriller, and sprouting keywork, it fought back to become the Romantic recorder.

Romantic music presented a challenge to the recorder. Faced with massive orchestras and modern pianos, the recorder had to fight to be heard, and rather than become larger, it became smaller.

In the 19th-century, an amateur musician could play decidedly romantic music on several different types of duct flute, depending on where he was. In Paris there were the flageolet, the galoubet, or even the flûte harmonique, in London the patent single, double or even triple flageolet, in Vienna the Wiener flageolet, csakan, flûte douce or Flötuse.

The csakan, in effect a keyed recorder, first appeared around 1807 in Budapest and was probably the invention of Anton Heberle, with a range of 2 octaves and a fifth. By 1815 up to 13 keys might be added, along with a tuning-slide and a device for narrowing the thumb-hole, and the csakan continued to be played until the turn of the 20th century. Conrad Mollenhauer, still a very successful firm of recorder makers, started by making csakans and flageolets in the 19th century.

The Recorder in the 20th century. At the end of the Victorian era, musical interest, for possibly the first time, began to spread backwards as well as forwards.

The mainstream early music revival began with the re-discovery of Bach by Mendelssohn, and the Arts and Crafts movement, with their interest in everything renaissance, copied an imaginary ideal of the courtly life as depicted in art, and represented by the surviving instruments of the period.

Received opinion has it that Arnold Dolmetsch was wholly responsible for this revival, but in fact copies of historical recorders were already being made and played on the continent, and the promotion of the recorder as an educational instrument in Germany by Peter Harlan soon resulted in the new techniques of injection moulding and mass production being applied to what appeared to be a very simple product.

The lack of understanding of the instrument, and imprecise manufacturing methods, fuelled by the adoption of the recorder by the German youth movements of the 1930's, meant that millions of poor quality instruments were soon flooding the school and amateur market.

Many of us of a certain age will remember a particularly hideous and ubiquitous descant in a pale wood with a plastic beak, and, of all things, a British Standards kite mark on the back, which could hardly have been described as capable of producing music in any shape or form!

The recorder was saved as a serious instrument by two notable 20th Century musicians, David Munrow and Frans Bruggen, who had been respectively promoted by the mainstream recorder labels, EMI and Telefunken. Both good looking and charismatic, they played the recorder with serious intent!

David Munrow's sad death was a great loss, but Frans Bruggen inspired a generation of young players, and their first problem was – where to get a good recorder from? In the early days of the twentieth century, original instruments could be had for a few shillings from the umbrella stands in antique shops, [a friend of mine's aunt once bought an ivory Stanesby flute from one], but as these began to be snapped up by players and museums, the problem of supply became acute. Cue Fred Morgan.

Fred quickly became a legend. Going back to source for his inspiration, he travelled widely through Europe, examining and measuring original instruments. Working in The Hague and then from the Australian outback, he supplied copies of original recorders to Frans Bruggen and his pupils that were every bit as good as those he had measured in museums.

Quickly acquiring a waiting list many years long, he nevertheless found time to run a series of classes in Holland where he passed on his experience to a new generation of makers, many of whom are still working today. Later, Alec Loretto ran classes in recorder-making in Austria which some of the younger makers attended.

Even though Fred suffered an untimely death, this generosity ensured that his rediscovered techniques of recorder making were passed on. [I must put a plug in here for the book 'Recorders Based on Historical Models', compiled by Gisela Rothe and published by Mollenhauer, which is a collection of memoirs and writings by Fred – essential reading for an impression of a recorder maker's life].

Now, in the 21st century, what is driving the recorder on? The recorder world [or the world of any instrument] is a cycle, and the components of that cycle are the composers, the publishers, the performers, the students, the teachers, the retailers, the makers and the audience, and it was probably remarkably similar in earlier times. We all work with each other, and without any one of these the cycle collapses.

There is still a great deal of conservatism in the recorder world, with hair splitting arguments over what might have been performance practice 300 years ago occupying the minds of learned academics, but there is also a radical cutting edge.

The use of the recorder as an educational instrument is still flourishing despite its unfortunate beginnings, and the contemporary world has embraced it as the most simple, and therefore the most flexible of instruments, giving it new music using extended techniques, electronics and computers.

Stichting Blokfluit, a Dutch database of recorder music, lists 5017 contemporary compositions for recorder at March 19th, 2009, and although professional students still go through the obligatory initiation of Handel and Telemann, contemporary performance is seen as absolutely essential to their training. Major German manufacturers have developed contemporary keyed recorders in collaboration with individual makers, and music is now being written than can only be played using one of these instruments.

On an amateur level, the recorder orchestra is flourishing with arrangements of all parts of the classical repertoire being published, for an instrumentation that spans more than 5 octaves from garklein to sub-contra great bass in F, and in the U.K. the National Youth Recorder Orchestra, sponsored by the Society of Recorder Players, will soon be 10 years old!

In fact it can probably be said that, with the exception of choral singing, the recorder now probably gives more pleasure to more people of a certain age than any other practical musical activity.

I have been fortunate to live through most of the new renaissance of the recorder, and it has been a fascinating journey. I have a vision that one day in the future someone on a package holiday will play Handel on one of my recorders under a binary sun at the far side of the galaxy. Homo Sapiens, recorder exporters to the Universe!

The Birth of a Recorder.

Recorders do not make themselves, and do not grow on trees, so a player must get his instruments from a shop, the Internet, his great aunt, or from a recorder maker like me.

All makers try very hard to raise our recorders properly with good habits, a sunny temperament and some of our own personality, but inevitably there will come a time, as with every parent, when you just have to let go, and the recorder will pass to a new owner – from the maker who nurtured it into life from some unprepossessing bits of a tree, to a new home – and it could be yours!

Think back to the day you bought your first recorder from a music shop, probably accompanied by your mum. It may have been bright and shiny with a glossy coat, but in the eyes of the person behind the counter it was just a commodity, sold off the shelf like one from a cage full of puppies at a pet supermarket, that in all probability had no serious love and attention given to it since it left its mother!

Buying a recorder from the maker is like visiting a specialist breeder. The product goes from someone who cares very much for it, straight to someone else who would like to care very much for it. However, all we can do is pass on the instrument, not the techniques of care that went with it, and unlike a gamba or a spinet, which will be lovingly preserved in a case or a humidity-controlled music room, it will spend the whole of its life being spat into! So, sooner or later, it will misbehave and chew up the Telemann. Now it's up to you to train it, feed it, take it out for walks, so that it becomes as much 'man's best friend' as any ex-Battersea mongrel.

**!!BEAR IN MIND THAT ANY GUARANTEE YOU HAVE, OR FEEL THAT YOU HAVE WITH YOUR RECORDER MAKER WILL REQUIRE A GREAT DEAL OF SMOOTH TALKING TO RETRIEVE IF YOU PASS THIS POINT, AND THE AUTHOR TAKES NO RESPONSIBILITY! –
IF IN DOUBT, PRACTISE FIRST!!**

CHAPTER 2

Basic Training

Keeping it's coat shiny.

It wasn't until I bought my first good saxophone that I realised just what an effect the purchase of a new instrument can have. Until then the recorders in my workshop had just been things I lived with every day, usually covered in a fine layer of dust until polished up for exhibition, but now I was facing this beautiful, silver, mechanical marvel and I WANTED IT!!!Could it be that my customers felt the same? Well of course they did! They wanted to fall in love with the instrument that would express their music to the world, and they wanted it to look pretty.

The external finish on recorders varies widely depending on the maker/factory that they came from. Starting at the bottom, makers of plastic instruments have either said 'this is plastic –learn to love it' or 'well it may be plastic but from a distance let's try and pretend it's not' and have used various wood look-alike finishes. There's not a lot you can do with it, except, like a damp muddy pooch, give it a good soak occasionally in a bucket of warm, soapy water and a thorough rinse under the tap.

Cheaper wooden recorders will have some sort of spray-on varnish, which will easily become chipped and scratched. If you can't live with this then treat it like your car. Rub it down with very fine wet and dry emery paper or steel wool, and then spray it with cellulose lacquer, either clear, or as close to the colour as you can find. Some friends of mine make a small profit by buying mass produced wooden recorders from E-bay, stripping off the varnish, delivering a few well aimed blows with a battle-axe or similar, and then selling them at a premium to medieval re-enactors who absolutely love the battle-scarred finish. You can certainly do a complete varnish removal job with paint stripper or sandpaper if you like, and you may well find a very nice piece of pear wood or maple beneath, but don't take too much thickness off the wood or you might change the tuning.

High-end recorders will have a more subtle finish involving various chemical stains, or a natural wood finish with oil or wax to resist finger dirt. At its simplest, if a recorder is black, then the wood will be either blackwood or ebony, and there will most likely be no external finish. If it's really mucky, clean it off with the finest grade of steel wool, OOOO, and then use either an oily cloth, or wax-polish it.This also applies to rosewoods, although you can also find a varnished finish on these.

A digression on oils. *Those you will mostly come across are almond oil, linseed oil, jojoba oil and tung oil. Almond oil does not dry, and is therefore used mostly for the bore. The others dry, and should not be used in the bore as they can build up to give a nasty, crusty, patina that may get into the fingerholes, and could affect the tuning. You can use a drying oil on the outside, but be very careful not to leave an accumulation in the fingerholes. Drying oils* will not 'dry' on a recorder made from oily woods such as blackwood, or one that has been impregnated with paraffin wax. They will just make a sticky mess, which you will have to clean off with white spirit or similar.

Boxwood recorders come in two sorts, real boxwood [buxus sempervirens] and fake [various yellow hardwoods from the tropics]. It can be difficult to tell them apart, but it is unlikely that a hand-maker will use anything other than real European boxwood. Boxwood will often be stained or dyed in various shades of red/brown, and once again it is difficult to tell between the two methods. Traditional acid-staining travels into the surface of the wood, and is often uneven in colour, but because this follows the natural grain of the wood, it is not unpleasing to look at. The recorder will probably have been soaked in linseed oil, and this will also have penetrated the wood and dried. Minor scuffs on an acid-stained recorder can be treated with OOOO wire wool, as removing a small part of the surface will not penetrate the stain. The finish can be restored with an oily cloth to leave a thin coat [see note above], or wax polished.

Some hand-makers use an external stain. This barely penetrates the wood surface, and is all too easily removed, so do not use wire wool or you will very quickly end up with a patchy yellow and brown finish. I must confess that I am not quite sure how to restore the finish here, so I tend to leave well alone. Some German high-end factory models also use a surface stain that seems to have been applied with a sponge or similar. Once again, this can be easily damaged. You can identify these stains as they are evenly distributed, and do not follow the grain of the wood.

Renaissance recorders will probably be made of maple or fruitwood of some sort. This wood will be softer and more easily damaged than boxwood or tropical hardwoods, so a careful wipe with white spirit followed by oil or wax polish is all you should try.

Maintaining the inner pet – cleaning the bore.

At school I was taught that we are essentially a tube on legs. What goes in at one end gives us energy to walk around and find other tubes on legs to make more little tubes with, so we have to keep it well fed! We call our recorder tube a 'bore', and a healthy bore means a bouncy bore operating on all harmonics! So let's have a look inside.

A healthy bore, if seen in a strong light, will be nicely polished and oiled from end to end, with no fluffy bits. As you can imagine, the vibrating air column does not like fluffy, spiky, or sharp edges, and works a lot better without them.

I once traumatised the Society of Recorder Players by suggesting that wire wool on the end of an electric drill could be used to polish bores! I still stand by that particular method, but it should be done carefully, and I will describe it later.

The places where you are most likely to encounter sharp, fluffy or spiky bits are in the fingerholes, so have a good look down them in a strong light. A fingerhole has two edges, inside and out, and between is a surface of wood that can collect oil, sweat, fluff and general grime. Go to a home-brewing shop and buy a very thin nylon bottlebrush, the sort that is used for cleaning out plastic tubing. Cut it down to 5 cm or so and use it to clean out the fingerholes. Afterwards use cotton buds with alcohol to really clean the sides.

Basic Training

All this is non-invasive, but a great improvement to the tone can often be made by smoothing off the sharp corner of the hole as it meets the outside of the recorder, and actively polishing the fingerholes. You can smooth the fingerhole corners with a cone of fine abrasive paper, but not to excess or the pitch may rise.

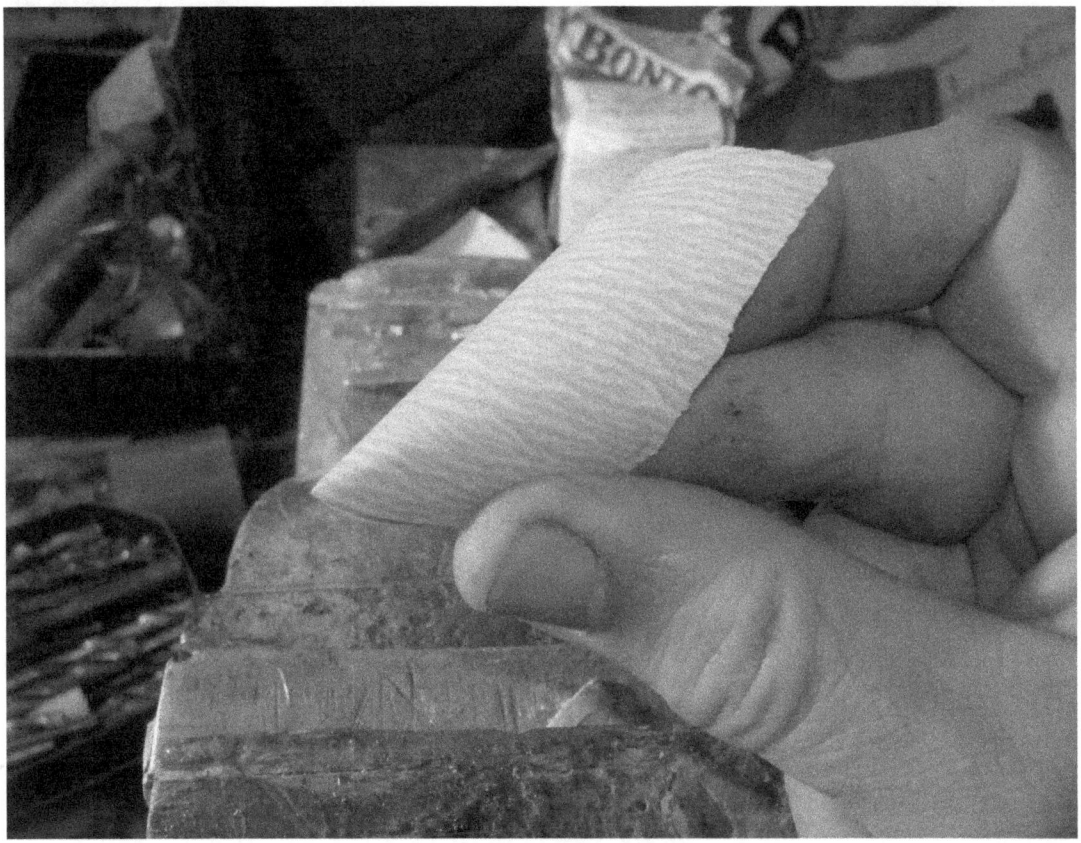

Fig. 1-Abrasive paper cone – 220 grade dry lubricated paper is best.

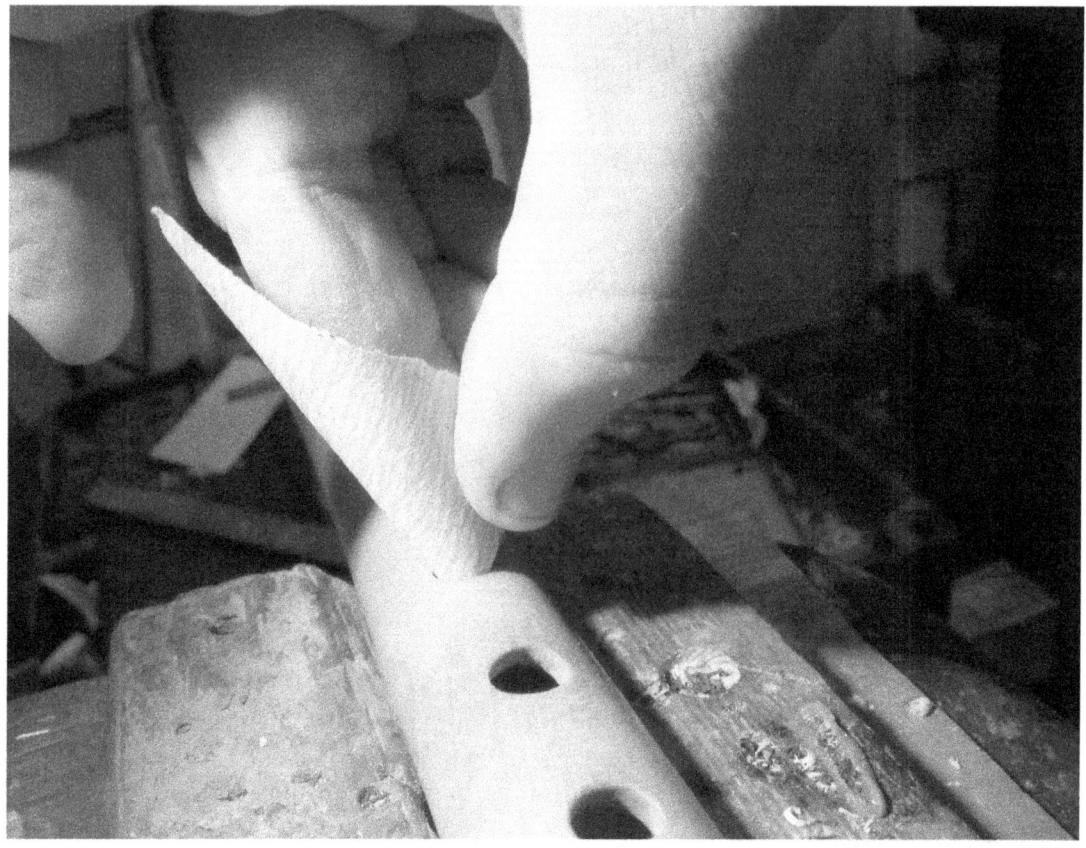

Fig. 2 – Using the abrasive paper cone

Placing the cone in the fingerholes as shown, lightly rotate the paper with a circular motion, and finish with some fine steel wool. Use a bottle brush to clean any bits out of the bore, and polish the hole inside by hand with some 400 grit paper wound round a drill bit [but **not** in the aforementioned electric drill] that is small enough to go in the hole and has been dunked in some almond oil, but be very careful not to enlarge it.

Inside the bore, the best gentle cleaning method is with a larger bottlebrush. [These can be purchased at specialist recorder shops, or just from your local kitchen suppliers.] This can also be used to oil the bore, dribble some oil on the brush and work it up and down inside the recorder

Basic Training

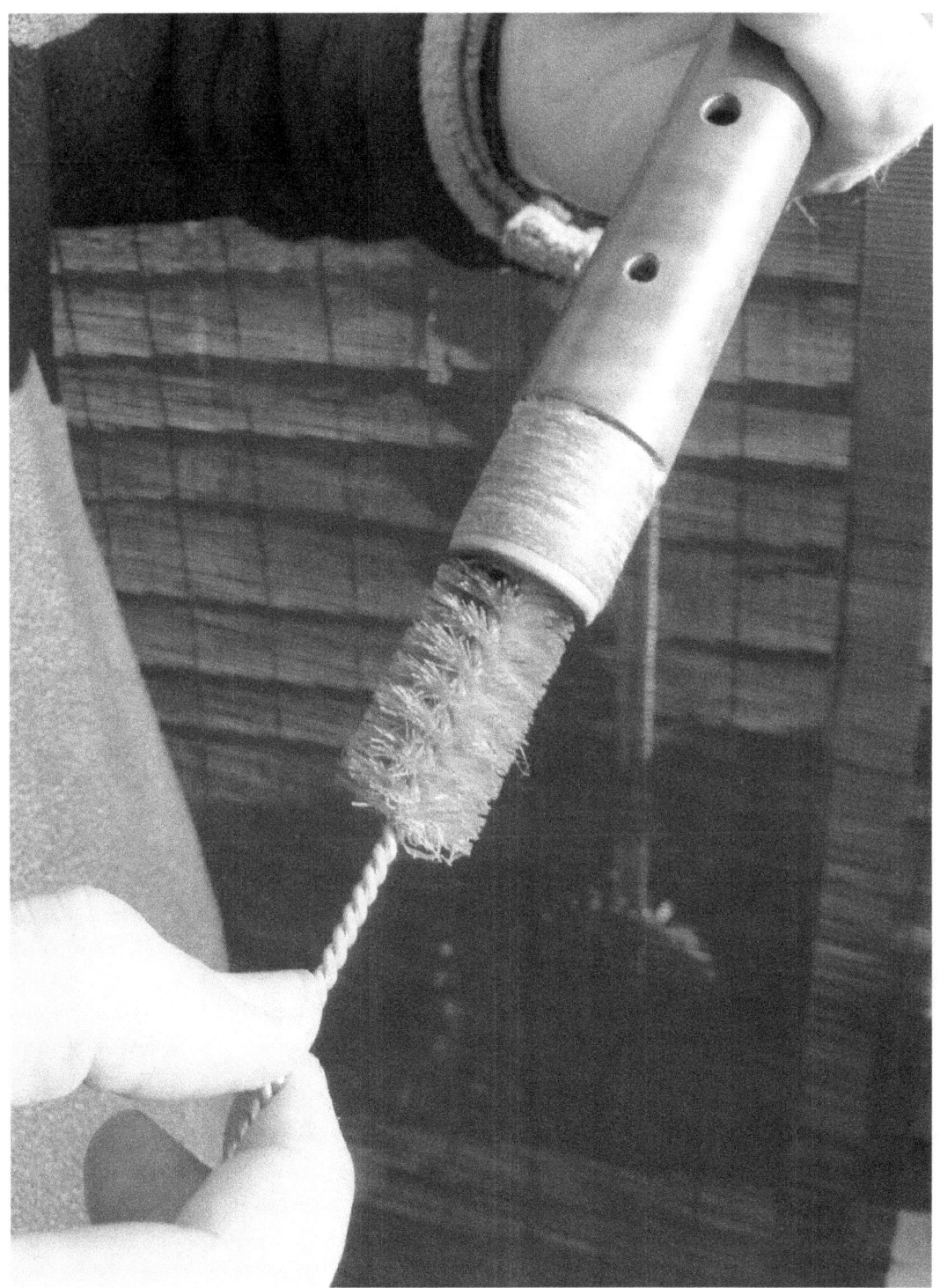

Fig. 3 - Using a bottlebrush to clean and oil the bore.

The notorious Cranmore 'wire wool on the end of an electric drill' method can be used if the surface of the bore is very rough, although not to excess or this will change the bore characteristics and the tuning. I use it on all my recorders for polishing the bore, and although it seems drastic, it does work. Get a bicycle spoke, or similar length of fairly rigid wire, then either bend a loop into the end or cut a slot with a fine hacksaw, and thread a hank of medium grade steel wool [1 or 2] into it.

Fig. 4 -Steel wool on a length of wire

Grip the end of the wire in the drill chuck [nb; I am talking a domestic cordless drill here, not an industrial hammer job], and hold each joint in one hand with the drill in the other. Insert the steel wool before switching on, and move the rotating steel wool up and down the bore [you can clean the headjoint with the block removed, but **not** above the window]. Start with the foot joint and add steel wool at a greater thickness for the centre and head, but be careful not to use too much of a thickness or it might jam in the bore. **Always** insert the wire wool into the bore before switching on the drill, or it will thrash wildly out of control, and switch off while taking it out, for the same reason.

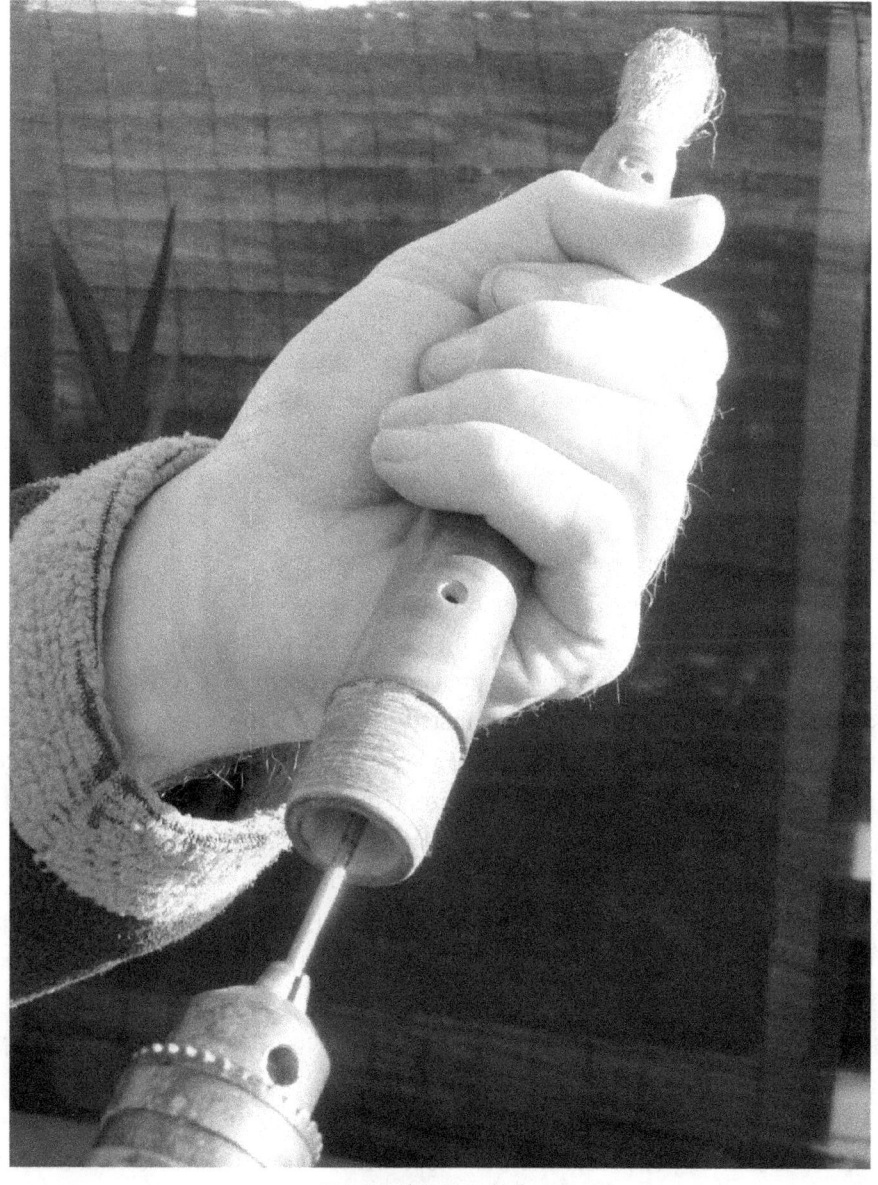

Fig. 5 - Cleaning the bore

This is NOT a technique to be repeated too often, and should only be used on instruments that have been neglected or have a really dirty or rough bore. If in doubt, practise first on an old instrument.

When you have smoothed the bore to your satisfaction, use some recorder oil on a bottlebrush, or if the wood seems very dry, you can immerse the centre joint and foot joint for a day in an oil bath.

The head joint [without the block!] can be immersed, but all traces of oil must be removed from the block socket before the block is replaced. Stand it upright, stuff the block socket with paper towel, and let it stand for a day or two. Oily blocks can be cleaned with acetone or some other oil solvent. Soak the block for a few minutes, and all that unwanted oil will be washed out into solution or carried deep into the wood where it can do no harm.

Fettling the Joints.

As young, shining, feisty recorder players, we all take our joints totally for granted, and bob happily down to the pub of a lunchtime with young Rover bouncing from one lamppost to another, but fast forward ten years or more and that annoying achiness of a morning doesn't quite wear off before the first pint goes down, and Rover would rather slump under the table than catalogue doggies' bottoms. In much the same way, the joints on a recorder will wear out, but it is rather easier to give them a new lease of life than to have a hip replacement! Joints come in three packages;

Plastic. Despite the impression that plastic is unchanging, the dimensions of these very close fitting joints can alter. If too loose, they can be packed with joint grease, but if too tight it is probably due to a very thin but sticky layer of dirt, grease etc. Clean off the tenon with a cloth and white spirit, and get into the mortise with cotton buds. Apply some clean joint grease and re-assemble.

Cork. Cork is nearly always found on wooden instruments from the larger workshops, and often sits in recessed sockets on the centre joint. If the joint is too loose, the cork can be expanded by gently heating it with a low flame while rotating the joint. Be careful not to burn it – or the wood! If too tight, the first thing to check is that the tightness is in the cork, and not in the shoulders of the socket holding it in place. If the latter, you will have to sand the wood down and then replace the cork.

If you have a lathe, mount the centre joint in it on a mandrel [a piece of turned wood that fits snugly in the top end of the centre joint], and remove the cork using a parting tool or very coarse abrasive. Reduce the shoulders of the socket with abrasive until you have about a 0.25mm clearance all round when inserted into the mortise. If you don't have a lathe, you will just have to cut the cork out with a scalpel, and reduce the shoulders manually.

To replace the cork, you first have to find some in sheet form, although you might consider using thread instead. The easiest source is your local bicycle shop, which should have cork handlebar tape. Cut a rectangle that just fits into your socket, clean the surface thoroughly with alcohol, and use contact adhesive to glue it in. Try and make it too thick so it can be adjusted later, and hold it in place with some thin rubber bands until set. Sand to fit, and use joint grease, as the new cork surface will be very dry.

Thread. All original recorders and most of those from hand-makers will have threaded joints, which may or may not sit in a socket on the tenon. These will tend to disintegrate with time, but are easily fixed. If the joint is too loose, wind some extra thread round it, preferably of a different colour from the original so that you can identify it and remove it later. I just use ordinary polyester sewing thread, but by all means use something more authentic if you like. The way to lay the thread so that it holds together is to use a technique that Boy Scouts call a whipping. Lay a loop of thread along the joint surface so that the end of the loop is lying above the tenon on the recorder body, and the free ends are below it. Wind the thread from your spool round the tenon towards the loop to bind it to the surface. When you have reached the required thickness, finish at the shoulder of the tenon, cut the thread and feed the loose end through the loop. You should now have two free ends, one above the tenon through the loop, and one hanging below which passes under the wound thread to the loop. Pull this one tight and your loop and the first free end will be drawn under the windings and secured. If the joint is too tight, the thread is best replaced.

To completely replace the thread I do the following.
- Make sure that the tenon is oil-free with about 0.5mm clearance between tenon and mortise.
- Start to wind the thread with the whipping technique as described above.
- After a few layers of thread have been applied, 'spot-weld' the thread to the wood with thin superglue.
- Complete the whipping using a chaotic winding which is far more likely to stay together than laying the threads neatly next to each other.
- When you have reached the required thickness, finish the whipping by drawing through the loose end.
- Spot-weld the entire body of the thread with superglue to hold it together.
- Soak the thread in molten wax of some sort. Beeswax will be authentic but can be very sticky. I use paraffin [candle] wax, which I dribble onto the thread, and then warm in a candle flame to allow it to soak in. Immediately assemble the joint to squeeze out the excess. This can give rather hard joint, so use a bit of almond oil to soften the top surface.
- If you make the joint a little loose, and then apply a few turns of a different colour to tighten it, these can be easily removed at a later date if necessary.

Exploring the Voicing.

Rather like being asked to examine the teeth of a Rottweiler or deliver a suppository to a Jack Russell – 'All hope abandon ye who enter here'. However, some intrepid owners have been to hell and back and lived to tell the tale, so, with no responsibility accepted, here is a guide to recorder voicing and how to fix it.

I have been voicing recorders for 30 years and I still don't really understand it. All I do know is that the sound that comes out of your column of air is a truly international one. All parts of the tube contribute, and all of them have to be considered. A mistake that I often made, as presumably did everyone else, was to look for a magic bullet that will conquer all the faults in one fell swoop. [What is a fell swoop? – sounds a bit like bog snorkelling!]. The fact is that, in constructing a voicing, you are balancing surfaces, angles, directions, air flows, air pressures, any one of which could profoundly disturb the sound if you get it wrong, and in my case nearly all done by hand and eye, not in a computer controlled AutoCAD system. For example, at the windway exit there are many angles, surfaces and dimensions, all of which have to match, be symmetrical, and correctly guide the airflow.

It is in this situation that we come up against the engineering problem. No, not one that you solve with a lump hammer, but a problem with engineers, who profoundly believe that if you have the right information and sufficiently accurate machines, then any product can be turned out in any numbers with the same reproducibility as a Rolls Royce crankshaft, and that includes recorders.

I have seen an engineer spend an inordinate length of time setting up a massive computer controlled milling machine to make a cut that I do in 10 seconds with a hand operated scalpel, and the machine still got it wrong. A recorder looks to an engineer like an 'engineered' product, and in fact 90% of it can be treated as such, but the last 10% needs skill, experience, and, dare I say it, creativity to make it all come together.

I was once approached by a recorder 'factory' who asked me if I would be interested in voicing their high-end treble recorders, implying that they meant to employ external hand-makers to apply the finishing touches. I duly voiced a couple of instruments and returned them, only to be told that they had been 'rejected'! By whom, I wondered, and on what basis? After a few enquiries I discovered that I was not the only maker who had been asked to submit instruments, and all of these had been lined up in front of a certain well-known player to be graded 1 to 5. However, was this to select the lucky maker who would be offered the job? Not at all. The winning recorder was to be measured by the most sophisticated instruments known to man, and then transferred to the computer, which would then make exact copies. Nice idea, but, in my opinion, not much hope of success. Each recorder is different, and the only entity capable of judging where the final cut has to be made is the recorder-maker him [or her]- self.

The voicing of a wooden recorder can, and will, go horribly wrong. It is, after all, designed within a small rectangular tube of two different woods, with different grain structures and absorbencies, which are then subjected to a continuous rain of body fluid. As nature abhors a vacuum, the ecosystem, which is subsequently created, will soon be colonised by all manner of flora, and occasionally fauna, and the wooden container will twist and turn and rise and fall with the seasons. Factory-produced recorders whose costing does not include a lengthy blowing-in session, attempt to forestall this by waterproofing the wood with paraffin wax, and by starting with a windway that is beyond the optimum specification for its function, thereby giving the floor and ceiling leeway to move.

Hand makers will always blow the recorder in for some time before letting it out of the workshop, and will re-voice it several times during the process. If the voicing has changed for the worse after use, it will most likely result in tightening of the sound with some edginess and extraneous noises, and this is nearly always caused by the block surface rising as it absorbs water, or a build up of deposits.

The Block. The idea of having a cedar block is that it can absorb a certain amount of water without expanding, and either disrupting the voicing or splitting the head joint, but this is not infallible. Various solutions have been tried, including chemical stabilisers, and the legendary part-ceramic block, which tended to disintegrate after some years of use.

If you are going to work on the block of a wooden recorder, it helps to be able to get it in and out, and this can be scary. Look down the windway into a strong light. Can you see the labium? Is the windway nice and symmetrical or do the corners seem rounded off? Are there little black things growing up from the top of the block or down from the windway roof? Is anything walking around or waving its legs at you? I still remember the noise made by an earwig as it hit the wall after a friend had sucked it out of a windway. If the answer to any of these is yes then the block might bear removal. If you have a friendly recorder maker round the corner then refer to him/her, but as these tend to be rarer than polar bears at the equator, why not have a go.

Planning is everything. Let the recorder dry out for a few days first, then find or turn a dowel with a diameter slightly smaller and about 10cm longer than the head joint bore, smooth off the end, and find a hammer! Take the head joint firmly in one hand, insert the dowel from the socket end, point the beak at your lap [with your legs together!], and hit the exposed end of the dowel with the hammer. One of three things will happen; the block will come out and fall into your lap –well done! – The block will come halfway out - hit it again – or the block will not shift. In the last case try hitting the dowel harder, but if there is absolutely no movement it is best to leave the recorder for a week to dry out thoroughly and try again. If you still have no success refer to your local recorder maker.

I once tried to remove the block from a very precious baroque original. The block came out halfway and then stuck fast. I only had two options; leave the block where it was and live with the recorder on display for a hundred years with a sign saying 'Unplayable due to failed block removal by Tim Cranmore', or hit it hard. Twenty minutes later, when I had stopped shaking and had already mentally booked my one-way ticket to Outer Mongolia to spend the rest of my life as a monk, I hit it hard, and luckily for me the block flew out without splitting the headjoint from end to end.

Blocks you might find.

Tapered block – fits into a tapered socket in the head joint – easy to remove and replace but not too easy to adjust backwards and forwards
Parallel block – fits into a parallel socket in the head joint. Not easy to remove or replace, but can be easily adjusted backwards and forwards
Socketted block – fits into a section of the bore that is larger than the sounding bore, but fits against a shoulder in the bore and cannot be easily moved beyond that.
Two part block – comes in three versions:
1. A cedar block with the centre removed and replaced with another cylinder of cedar with flexible cement between the two. Designed to prevent expansion of the block

2. A cedar block in two parts with a square section glued into a groove, which has been machined into the top surface of the block and forms the upstand. A means to speed up and simplify block production.
3. A cedar block with a ceramic insert as the windway floor intended to absorb excess moisture. These are no longer used as they have tended to disintegrate with time, and the whole block usually needs replacing.

Synthetic blocks are now coming into use even in expensive instruments. I have not yet handled one so have no opinion on them.

Windway blockages you might find.
1. Food, spit, lipstick, cigarette smoke; need I go on? – Recorder makers occasionally need a strong stomach.
2. Fungus, often seen as a series of pinhead size lumps which you can feel with a fingertip inserted into the windway.
3. Paraffin wax – usually seen in mass-produced recorders that have been left in the sun.
4. Fluff from those abominable fluffy cleaning sticks that used to be standard equipment with every new recorder.

Any, or all, of these may be on both the windway and the block, but can be cleaned off with care, using mechanical or solvent means.

I once got into a great deal of trouble by drawing attention to the deposits of food that were seriously compromising the tone of a plastic descant in a festival at which I was adjudicating. The boy's mother nearly killed me, and I was never asked back!

Block cleaning.

Food etc. deposits really need removing, and as they will be mostly at the blowing end, there is less possibility of making unwanted changes to the voicing. Try a soft toothbrush under a stream of warm water, or if baked hard, use fine steel wool or a scalpel blade on the dry block. The pinhead fungus will be distributed all along the block surface, and the best means of removal is gentle scraping with a scalpel blade. Always scrape **away** from the windway exit so as to not touch the end chamfer. Some people will say that a certain amount of slime on the block surface helps spit to slip through easily and avoids blocking, but if the windway size has been reduced then it needs to go.

Basic Training

Windway-cleaning.

Not so easy! Have a look at the wind channel of a clean recorder with a strong light, and become familiar with the shape that both the block and the windway should be. In a decent instrument, both windway roof and the block surface will have been made with a slight longitudinal concavity. The chamber created between the two accelerates the airflow so that is it at its fastest when it exits from the windway. You can see it by carefully laying a straight edge such as a 6" steel rule along the block surface or along the windway. The rule should only make contact at the very ends. [See fig. 16]. If there is a bit of a 'hill' in the middle of either, then the wood may have moved, and you may feel like adjusting it yourself if you are feeling particularly brave, and I will cover this later. However, just restoring the windway to its default manufactured state must also be done very carefully, as you don't want to remove any of the original wood unless you are entering the uncharted waters of DIY voicing.

Much talk is often made about cotton buds and alcohol, and by all means try these first, but they are very gentle, and probably won't touch most deposits.

Hard blockages will probably be fungus, food or paraffin wax. Wax can be very difficult to remove as it does not dissolve in any solvent generally available at the hardware shop, so it is better to scrape it out, but to start with, try a soft toothbrush with the bristles cut down to 5mm or so, and don't worry about just using warm, soapy water with it. After all, the windway is used to having its daily bath, and don't forget to clean under the labium as the corners here will often be mucky as well.

For deposits that won't shift, you can use a small file with the end ground down to a square edge at one end, a curved edge at the other, and the file serrations smoothed off. [See fig.15]. This tool will be useful to get right into the corners of the windway, but be very conscious of the difference in 'feel' between muck and wood, especially at the south end of the windway. For the centre of the windway, a small bit of fine steel wool on a fingertip will do the job.

While you are in cleaning mode have a look at the window. You will often find that the corners of the window exhibit the same gunge as the windway, so try a toothbrush again but with longer bristles, or scrape them away with a scalpel. If a fluffy cleaner has been used there will also be bits of fluff embedded everywhere. [ps. If you have one of these, please dispose of it immediately so that mankind can never use it again!]. These will interfere with the air stream by vibrating in it, and you can spend a lot of time individually removing them!

Block replacement

What comes out must go in? – Not necessarily, especially if the block has come from a parallel socket, when you may well find that the end of the block appears not to fit the hole it came out of. When re-fitting a block it is best if you have a sliding fit, so that force need not be used when replacing it.

A tight block can be reduced in size either with abrasive paper or with a scraper or scalpel blade. If it goes in part of the way then sticks, you should be able to see the sticking points as polished areas on the round section of the block after you have taken it out again. These can be selectively sandpapered or scraped down and the block tried several times, hopefully going in further each time. I prefer a sliding fit with a good shove from the thumb, and maybe a tap from a block hammer for the last 0,5mm or so.

Rubbing a wax candle along the rounded section can make insertion easier by lubricating the block. If the block won't go back in at all, you will have to reduce its size at the south end [rounded section only] until it starts to enter. Don't force it at any point or you risk splitting the beak. With the block in place, look down the windway again. If you have a nice view of the labium then all may be well, if not, refer to the next chapter.

CHAPTER 3

Advanced Training

If you have read the preceding chapter carefully, you will see that, rather like looking for fleas in a shaggy coat, I am encouraging you to look closely at your instrument – probably more closely than you have ever looked at it before. Now that you have had a really good look, we can have a go at some serious obedience training!

Recorders are made from wood – wood comes from trees – it is a dead but extremely complex skeleton of cellulose, lignin, spaces, tubes and fibres, and it cannot be guaranteed to be stable. Besides, as you grow as an owner, the recorder might no longer suit your technique, or you may begin to discover irritating behavioural traits that you didn't at first notice. Of course you can take it back to the maker, but he might have given up and become a bee-keeper, moved to Outer Mongolia after an unfortunate experience in a museum, gone mad after drilling too many holes, live the far side of the world, or just plain old passed away [RIP Fred!].

I have always tried to encourage players to buy from a maker that is local to them, not just for my sake, but also for the ease of just popping up the road for adjustments and for developing a personal relationship with him/her.

Really successful makers not only have good craftsmanship but also excellent personal skills [not to mention salesmanship, financial acuity and entrepreneurial talent].

It took me a long time to grow from being a typical defensive, reclusive young maker with a permanent scowl on my face, to managing to create at least a half decent relationship with my public. Makers that hide from their customers or who cannot take criticism soon lose their business.

Serious Recorder-Voicing.

Recorder voicing is sometimes referred to as a 'dark art'. Fred Morgan was once reckoned to be the only living maker who really understood the subject, but I think we are catching up. One thing to remember is that to ascribe all the properties of a recorder to the voicing alone is to lose oneself down a blind alley. Whether a recorder 'works' or not is the combined result of the voicing, the tuning, the bore, the wood, the 'blowing in' process etc. I have always described the construction of a recorder as a cyclical process. One aspect cannot be finished in isolation. All must be addressed in turn until the final product emerges, and even this cannot be thought of as 'final' until the instrument has been used for some time. Thus, the recorder must be voiced, tuned, cleaned, blown, voiced, tuned, cleaned, blown, voiced, tuned, cleaned, blown etc etc until finished to the maker's satisfaction.

This is not intended to be a course in recorder-voicing, but I will be giving away some secrets and short cuts that may be helpful to anyone who wants to have a go.

A successful recorder-voicing is all about symmetry, linearity, and balance. My life changed completely when I purchased my Alec Loretto – designed windway cutter, a machine that is used by many makers today. This mechanism allows the windway geometry to be varied in almost every dimension and angle, and once you have finalised your voicing, it can be reproduced every time. The voicing is the synthesis of the maker's ideas, so now I am going to encourage you to take a very hard look down your headjoint. If you are short-sighted take your glasses off [I remember the very first moment I did that just because my ears hurt – it was a revelation!], or use a magnifying glass.

On a well-made recorder you will see that the windway is curved laterally, but with a flatter curve than the bore itself. The windway should also be slightly concave along its length, and the lateral curve is maintained until the windway exit.

The windway entrance controls the volume of air entering, and also the pressure. The pressure and speed of the air needed to operate the voicing at its optimum needs to be just so, and in a well made recorder an increase in pressure at the windway entrance will raise the volume of the recorder as the whistle mechanism is made to work harder, but will not appreciably raise the pitch. The adjustable parameters at the windway entrance are the height after manufacture, and the height, width, and curve during manufacture. The reasons for a curved windway are often argued about, and I'm not sure that the advantages are immediately obvious, but baroque originals had them so we tend to expect it in our more expensive toys.

You should then concentrate your gaze on the windway exit, which is altogether a more complex arrangement. It is essential that the air exits in as symmetrical a way as possible so that it crosses the window in a cohesive and well-directed flow at the right speed and pressure for the voicing to operate effectively. Sounds difficult? Believe me it is!

Like you are doing now, I once had a good look at the voicing of a recorder and realised that there are at least 10 surfaces, 12 dimensions, 5 lines and 7 angles that have to be orientated with each other. As they say on takeoff – 'just take a moment to familiarise yourself with the interior of the cabin…..'.

The next drawing [Fig. 6] is of a baroque treble recorder voicing, which shows all of the details below;

The surfaces are;
- The north side of the window perpendicular to the windway [1]
- The south end of the block [2]
- The underlabium which joins the labium to the bore [3]
- The ramp which joins the labium to the external turning [4]
- The two sides of the window which confine the sides of the air stream [5]
- The top surface and sides of the windway [6]
- The top surface of the block [7]
- The top windway chamfer [8]
- The bottom windway chamfer [9].

The dimensions are;

- The height of the windway entrance. [10]
- The width of the windway entrance.. [11]
- The height of the windway exit. [12]
- The width of the windway exit.[13]
- The depth of the window. [14]
- The size of the two chamfers. [15]
- The thickness of the labium.[16]
- The length of the ramp[17]
- The height of the windway roof above the labium [the cut-up] [18]
- The height of the labium above the block surface. [19]
- The length of the underlabium. [20]
- The longitudinal position of the block within the bore [21]

The lines are;

- The labium itself, with which all the other lines are orientated [22]
- The four lines which comprise the edges of the top and bottom chamfers [23]

The angles are;

- The angle of approach of the windway. [24] –[And see fig. 21]
- The angle of both chamfers. [25]
- The angles of approach of both the labium and the underlabium [26] –[And see fig. 21]
- The angles made by the sides of the window as they come to the surface. [27]
- The angle made as the labium flares out to the surface. [28]

Not to mention the fact that many of these are curved, and that the curves have to match!

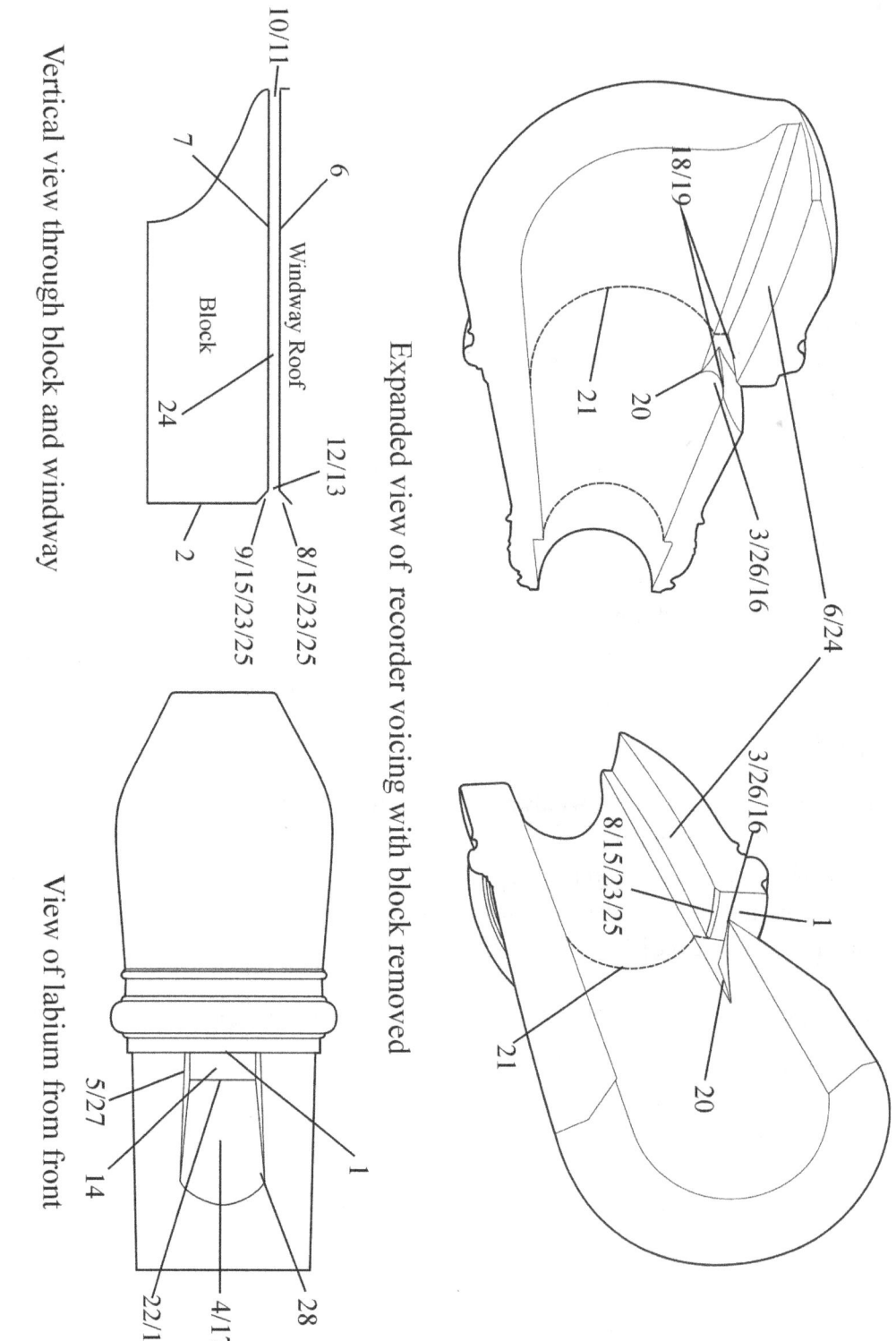

Fig. 6 - Various views of a recorder voicing to illustrate its geometry

I should point out that I hardly ever measure anything in the voicing. I just look at it. The eye is a marvellous comparator, and after many years I reckon that I can judge dimensions much better that any measuring instrument that I could possibly afford. I am often asked by engineers about fractions of a millimetre, and I have to admit that I really don't know!

You can see that the possible permutations of these lines and surfaces are overwhelming, but there are two things to remember. There is no such thing as a correct set-up, just one that works for you and the instrument, and that the greater the symmetry, the better the result. For example, the chamfers must be parallel to one another and to the block and windway. If they are not, the air stream will not exit correctly and will cross the window in a disturbed fashion.

To begin with I am only going to suggest that you try adjusting two of these, namely, the position of the block within the windway, and the relationship of the block surface to the labium. Later, we will move to processes that actually involve cutting into the main body of the recorder, but as these are by their very nature irreversible, I might ask you to sign a disclaimer first!

Looking and seeing

I sometimes suspect that we see what we want to see. Have you ever looked for a skylark that is singing merrily above [yes, we still have them in the Malvern Hills], and totally failed to spot it, then suddenly, when it is in view, you can't miss it. When I have asked players to look down a windway and describe what they see, they often seem to see nothing at all, or at least not what I am talking about.

Take your block out, and identify the north and south ends of it. Look down the empty headjoint and identify the windway and the labium. Now replace the block and see how they relate. You should be able to see the space between the labium and the windway roof, the labium itself, and the gap beneath the labium as seen along the top surface of the block. It is often said that the sign of a quality recorder is that the gap visible below the labium should not have any visible light, and this is often taken to mean that the block surface is so high that no direct light can be seen. However, if you think about it, you might not be able to see light if the windway slopes upwards [re-entrant], or if the centre of the underlabium is not coincident with the bore, but actually joins the bore some distance behind the labium itself.

A common problem with recorders after some use is that the block rises so that there is no direct sign of the labium, or it can only just be seen above the block surface. The symptoms are a scratchy tone, especially on the high notes, and a tendency to blockage with spit. If cleaning the block surface as covered previously does not reveal the labium, then the cure is often to lower the block surface so that the labium is visible once more.

Obedience Training for Recorders - *Tim Cranmore*

Block Adjustment

There are two ways to do this. The least invasive is to move the whole block without touching the top surface. To lower it, remove the block and place two strips of adhesive tape in the positions shown, either side of the upstand.

Fig. 7 - Using adhesive tape to lower the block

Try to re-insert the block. If this is successful you may well find that the south end of the block has been forced downwards. If the block will not go in because the addition of the tape makes it too tight, scrape or sand away the curved side of the block opposite from the windway and try again. Eventually you should find that the block will enter at a slightly different angle and the edge will be visible.

Occasionally you might see that the block appears too low, with a substantial gap seen beneath the labium, giving a windy sound. You can raise the block in the opposite way, by placing a piece of tape under the block at the south end, and by scraping material off at the two shoulders opposite the tape if it won't go back in.

Fig. 8 - Using adhesive tape to raise the block.

Actually changing the top surface of the block itself is, of course, permanent, but as a new block can be made, not too disastrous if you go wrong.

To adjust the block by sanding down the top surface requires that you have a very good idea of how that surface is to start with, so take a good look. I want you to notice especially the chamfer at the south end, its size, and the angle it makes with the block surface.

Fig. 9 - Block chamfer at south end of windway

You will need to reproduce that chamfer when you have re-finished the surface as some or all of it will be removed. Make a drawing or take a photograph.

Next, lay a straight edge along the block and notice any concavity. If there is none, then you might think about introducing one. I am only talking about a fraction of a millimetre in the centre, so that you can see light under the rule in the middle but so that it touches at both ends.

Advanced Training

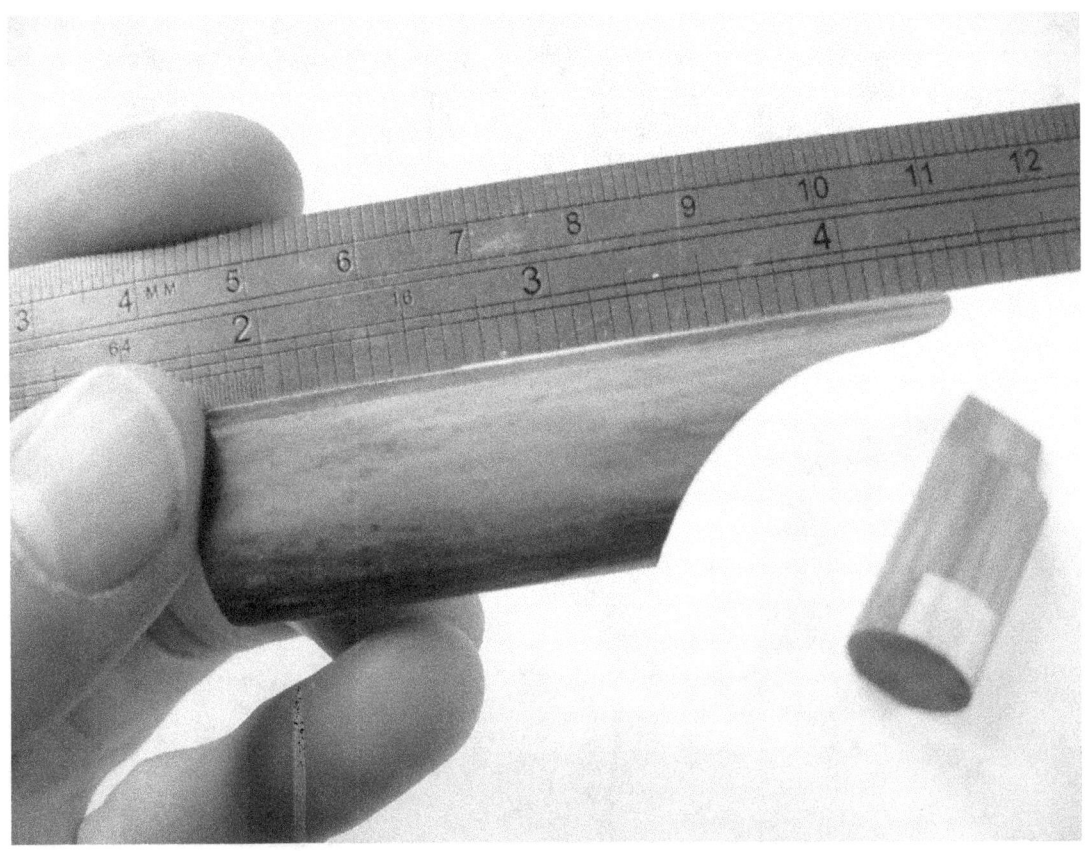

Fig. 10 - Checking the block concavity

If you don't have one, invest in a slim 6-inch steel rule that will also fit down a treble block socket to check the windway surface inside the recorder.

Find a small square block of wood and wrap some abrasive paper [220grade] round it, either holding it tightly with your fingers, or holding it in place with some double sided tape.

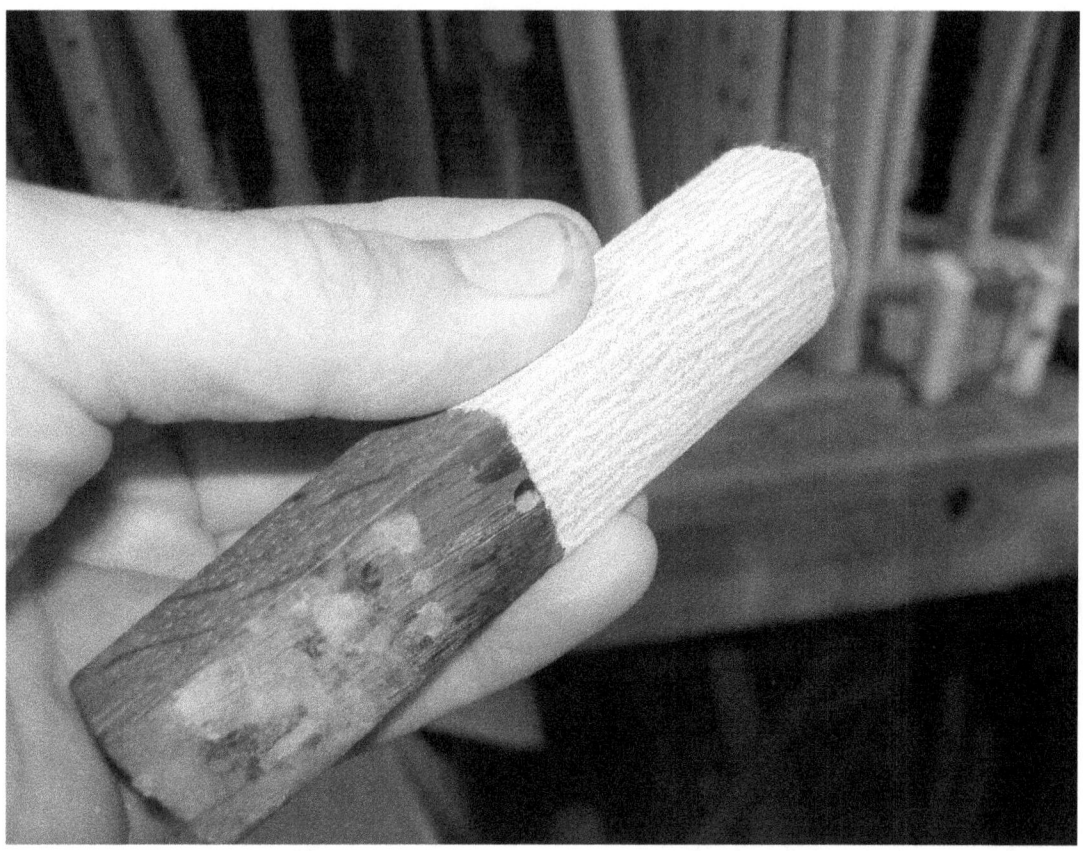

Fig. 11 – Sanding tool for block adjustment.

Using the sanding tool along the recorder block lengthways, abrade the cedar, rocking the tool slightly from side to side to allow for the curve of the windway. Abrade towards the north end of the block to lower the windway entrance, and towards the south end to lower the windway exit, but always keep the sanding surface flat to the block so it does not 'rock' over the ends.

Advanced Training

Fig. 12 – Using the sanding tool lengthways.

At the ends, use the existing chamfers as a guide, note that they should reduce in size equally if you are abrading the surface symmetrically. Check for concavity, and if it is not present, use the sanding tool **across** the block and with your thumb at the south end [as shown in figure 13] to prevent the abrasive from quite reaching the end of the block, and abrade the wood lengthways between the two ends of the block.

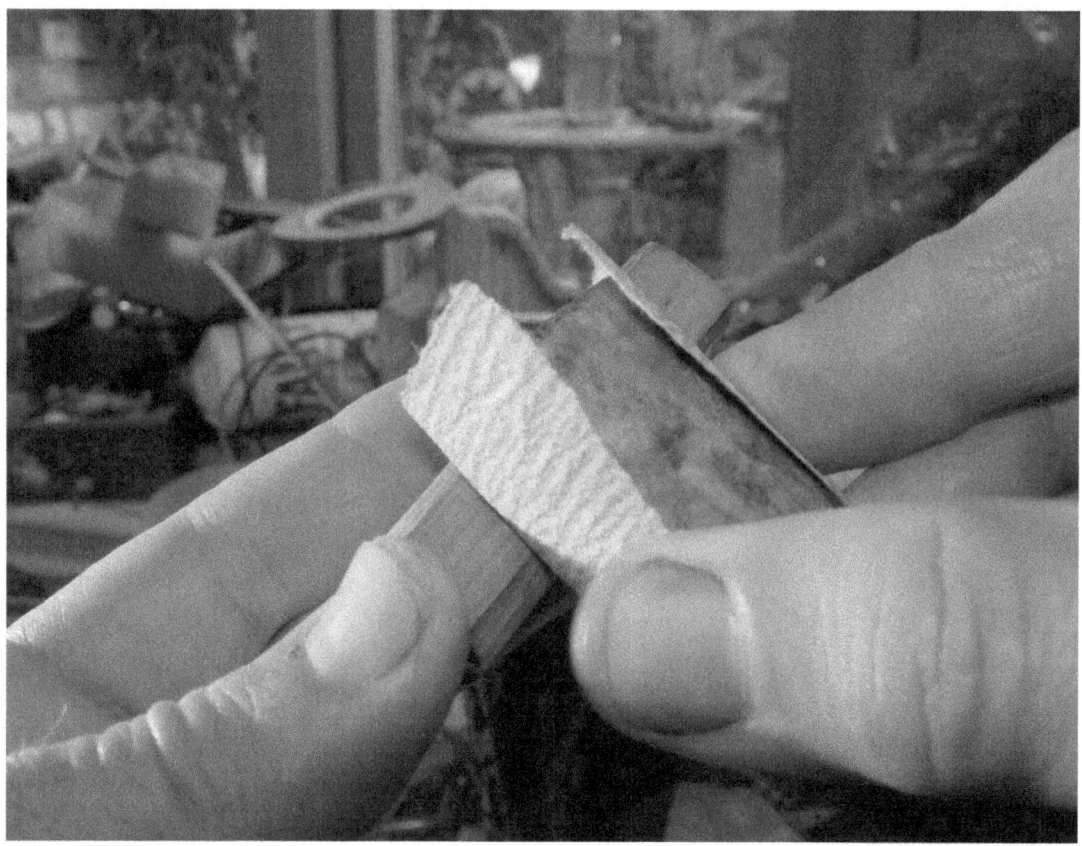

Fig.13 – Using the sanding tool across the block.

Now, using the sanding tool at an angle [figure 14], replace the chamfer, as it was originally, with fine abrasive [400 or similar], or experiment by trying the sound as you slowly restore it. Keep an eye out for symmetry, and size. Block chamfers can vary between almost non-existent to a couple of millimetres depending on the model and the taste of the maker. Always keep the paper flat against the tool surface by tensioning it with your fingers.

Advanced Training

Fig. 14 - Adjusting the block chamfer.

Sometimes I have found in cheaper instruments that no chamfer has been made in the first place, and just giving one to the block [or the windway] will transform the sound. Making a new block is always possible if you go too far, and some recorder makers, Moeck for example, will supply blocks that fit straight in without needing to adjust the sides, although the top surface will need finishing.

Replace the block in the headjoint and look for the labium. Blow the recorder and see if it has made a difference. Repeat the process if you feel it is necessary. If you want to raise the block again, use some adhesive tape as shown in figure 8.

The contemporary recorder developed by Maarten Helder, and now manufactured by Mollenhauer makes all this unnecessary. For example, the height of the block is adjustable using a screw thread mechanism so that the tone of the recorder can be changed from edgy to rounded as needed.

To investigate the effect of the block positioning, try leaving the block sticking out of the mouthpiece by a millimetre or so, or try and push it in further [but not using force or you may split the head]. See what effect this has on the tone. Sometimes you might like to change this position to suit the particular music being played at the time. Leaving the block standing out of the windway can give a breathy but fuller sound, whereas pushing it further in will give a tighter, brighter sound. If you find a position that you really like, then the beak and block can be re-profiled to match the new configuration.

CHAPTER 4

Really Major Surgery [WARNING – could be fatal!]

If by now you have the bug for DIY recorder adjustment, I am going to give an overview of all adjustments that can be made to the voicing and bore of a baroque recorder, and what might happen if you make them. There are no guarantees of success, and my first recommendation would be to go to EBay and invest in some tired out wooden instruments to practice on, or one of those ghastly mistakes that you bought 20 years ago and has sat at the back of the recorder rack ever since.

I have acquired a varied collection off EBay. Judging by the photo and the price [i.e. low] alone, I now have what I call my chest of recorder horrors, all of which were foisted on the public during the last 50 years or more as 'musical instruments' by various mass production facilities. They vary from early Bakelite jobs to American marching band plastic things that look like something from Whoville! I occasionally pass them out to a room full of teachers and challenge them to play a B in tune with each other.

It saddens me to think that these things were regularly passed out to primary school classes with the promise that they could be used to make beautiful music!

Having said that, I must admit that the plastic school recorder has vastly improved in recent years, but I still suspect [based on my own experience as a school recorder teacher] that the recorder is used in primary school as a filter mechanism. A box of assorted recorders is passed out to the class by the [usually unsalaried] recorder teacher, and after a few weeks it is obvious where the more talented musicians are. It is at this point that the [salaried] clarinet and flute teachers come nosing about asking innocently if anyone is any good- well we all want to show off our star pupils, don't we!- and before you know it your best players are swanning along the corridors with a gleaming, key-festooned orchestral instrument and seem to mysteriously 'quit' your class!

When these legions of clarinet and flute payers hit secondary school, there is, of course, very little for them to do, whereas those who have stuck with the recorder can at least play some very nice consort music!

The windway of a recorder is essentially a channel milled into the roof of the headjoint beak. It can point down into the bore and extend beyond the window as the underlabium on the same axis [best for mass production], or it can be parallel to the bore and change direction for the underlabium, more often seen nowadays in the better mass produced instruments, or it can slope slightly upwards, and be created entirely independently from the underlabium, which is milled separately or cut with an angled knife [the method probably used in baroque originals where the underlabium is usually very short and steep].

The height and width of windways vary considerably, but the basic rule is that the bigger the windway the more air you need to put down it to make it work, and the louder the recorder could be if the rest of the voicing is properly set up.

The advantage of a large windway is the range of manipulation of the sound available to the player, but disadvantages will include coarseness of tone, too much pitch variation with blowing, and a tendency for the player to pass out!

A small windway, with good focus, will give a much more precise sound, more pitch stability, and greater staying power per lungful, but can also be a bit of a straitjacket when it comes to expression.

If you want to open the windway of a recorder, the easy option would seem to be to just lower the block, and if it was too high in the first place this will give an improvement, but once the labium is visible any further lowering will quickly destroy the tone. You definitely need more space above the labium than below it. If the voicing still seems too tight, you might try to raise the roof at the south end. It may seem obvious to try to do this with abrasive paper on the end of a stick, but you could end up rounding off the end of the windway so try to make a scraper. I use a small, square file, ground down to a scraping edge at the end, with a curve that is slightly rounder than the windway profile at one end, and a square cut at the other.

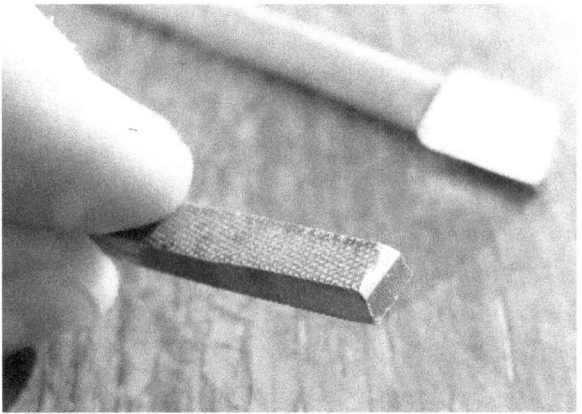

Windway scraper - square end

Windway scraper - curved end

Fig. 15 – Simple windway scraper ground from an old file.

The curved profile can be used in the centre of the windway, and the straight profile in the corners. This tool can also be used to introduce or adjust the windway concavity; however, it can only be used successfully if the grain of the wood is on your side. Once again, start by practising on an old recorder.

Try a very gentle test scrape along the centre of the windway towards the window. If the tool cuts neatly you are in luck; if it judders along and leaves a torn surface then the grain is working against you and there is very little you can do about it except use the abrasive-on-the-end-of-a-stick method.

This method is a lot less precise, and I would only use it if the choice is between ditching the recorder or not, but it can work if used with discretion and care.

Take a length of wood with a rectangular cross-section that fits into the windway with room to spare on either side, and profile it as near as possible to the lateral curve of the windway. Attach 220 grit abrasive paper with double-sided tape and use it on the windway as flat as possible so as to avoid rounding over the end, checking for concavity frequently.

For the centre section of the windway between the entrance and exit, you can also use a similar stick, but with a piece of firm sponge rubber attached to it. Cut a short section of rubber [about 1cm] the same width as the stick and about 5mm thick, and make a sandwich of abrasive, sponge rubber, and stick using double-sided tape. The sponge allows the abrasive to take the shape of the windway, but gives enough resistance to make sure that the abrasive works. Be very careful to use this tool between the ends of the windway only. You will not be able to use these tools in the corners of the windway, but a windway that is taller in the centre than at the sides will still work better than a windway that is too small everywhere.

If the grain is on your side, you can scrape gently and evenly towards and beyond the windway exit using your ground-down file. Start in the corners bringing them up equally, then scrape the centre maintaining the symmetry of the windway exit. Always have a mental picture of where you started, and as the windway height increases keep replacing the block and trying the tone, and don't forget that the windway has a beginning, a middle and an end. As you increase the capacity of the voicing, you may well have to increase the size of the air intake by lowering the north end of the block, and always check and maintain concavity on both windway and block surfaces.

By raising the roof at the windway exit, you will also have removed part or all of the top windway chamfer, so you really need to have made a record of it in advance. Take an ice-lolly stick or similar piece of thin, flat wood and trim it so that it fits neatly into the window with the same width. Put a blob of wax, plasticine, or some such on the end and press it into the top surface of the window. When you take it out you should have an impression of the top chamfer. Also, make a tool consisting of a small mirror on the end of a stick similar to a dentist's mirror. By introducing this in the bore underneath the end of the windway in a strong light, you should be able to see the chamfer through the window. You can also inspect the underlabium with the same tool.

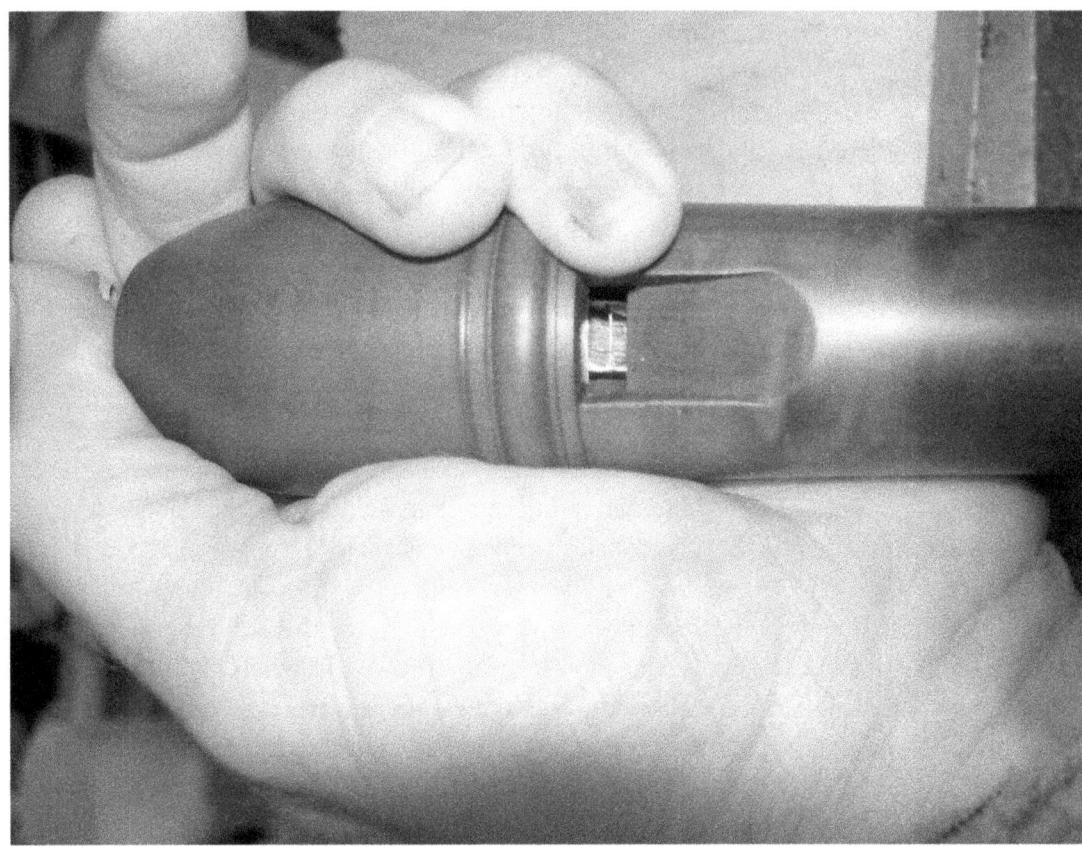

Fig.16 - Using a mirror-stick to inspect the chamfer and underlabium.

When you have finished re-profiling the windway exit, cut the top chamfer using a new scalpel blade. I find that no.10a is the best size and shape. The accuracy of this will depend on feel and experience. You can measure the chamfer as you go along by measuring the width of the shavings you are making, by looking at it in the mirror, or by taking further impressions. Bear in mind that this is an irreversible process. I have always used an angle of approx. 45 degrees for the chamfer, but there is nothing to stop you from experimenting at this point. Keep checking the tone of the recorder as you go along and see what a difference the top chamfer makes, and bear in mind that it must be balanced by the block chamfer, but they do not necessarily have to be the same size or angle, or even coincide at the same point in the bore, just be parallel to each other.

The Labium interrupts the airflow and introduces the acoustic vibration. A transverse wave is converted rather inefficiently into a longitudinal sound wave within the bore. The characteristics of the labium are its thickness, the vertical distance between the centre of the labium and the bore, and its length both on the outside of the recorder and also inside the bore [the underlabium]. The longer the underlabium, the more acute the angle between the outer and inner labium is going to be, and the angle that intercepts the air stream will effectively point more into the bore.

On mass-produced recorders the labium will be thicker as this is easier to make without too many disasters. The underlabium will be long as this is also easy to manufacture with one tool. On baroque originals the labium is usually thin, with a short underlabium, which was probably cut with an angled knife through the window.

Fig. 17 - Angled edge-cutting knife.

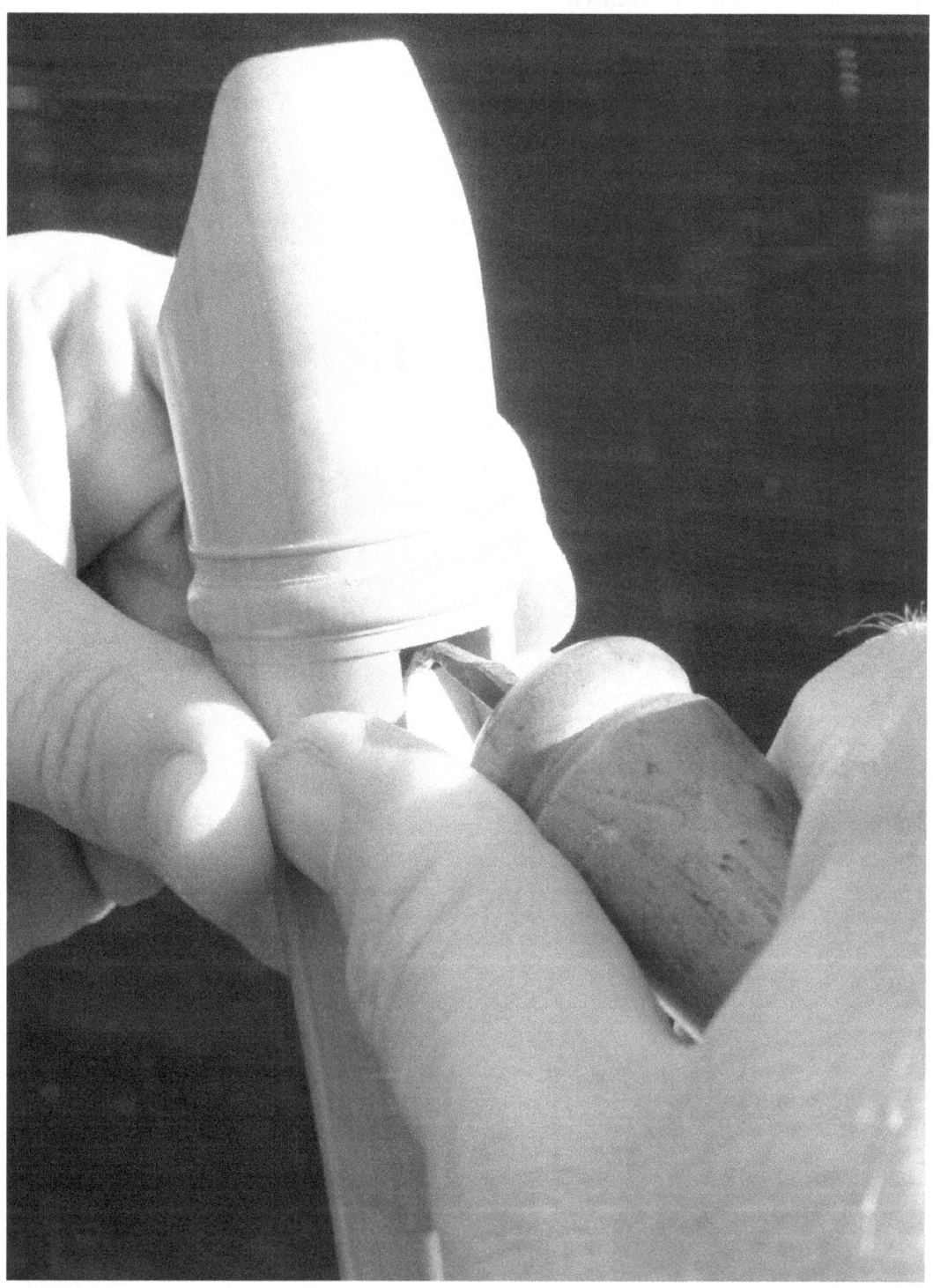

Fig. 18 - Using the edge-cutting knife through the window.

Really Major Surgery [WARNING – could be fatal!]

Fig.19 - Using the edge-cutting knife in the windway.

I have a theory that the angle at which the airflow hits the labium gives a particular character to the sound, and can explain the differences between a mass-produced instrument, and a hand made instrument using the above technique. The following diagram gives an idea of how this angle can be quite different depending on the length of the underlabium.

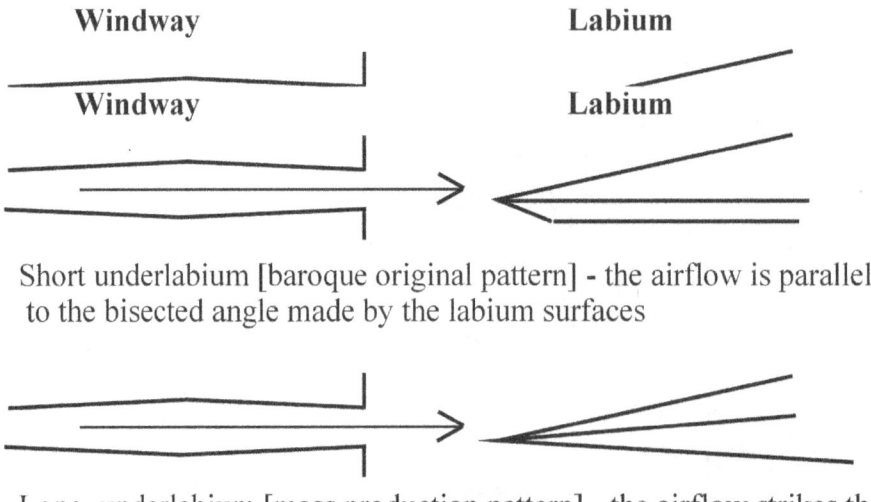

Short underlabium [baroque original pattern] - the airflow is parallel to the bisected angle made by the labium surfaces

Long underlabium [mass production pattern] - the airflow strikes the labium above the bisected angle made by the labium surfaces

Fig. 20 – Illustration of wind direction relating to labium angle.

The only experiment that you can really do with the labium is to cut it back with a scalpel and re-profile it with your scraper from the outside of the recorder. You can also do this to a certain extent if the labium is damaged. If the sound is rather tight then this can open it out, but fractions of a millimetre count here so be careful and be prepared to write the recorder off for the sake of curiosity.

On boxwood recorders the centre of the labium will sometimes lift as moisture is absorbed, and come out of line with the block surface and the windway roof. If you really feel that this is causing excessive windiness, you can encourage it back down by gently pressing the centre of the labium with a hot iron that is just short of 'burning' temperature.

CHAPTER 5

Tuning with the Bore and Fingerholes

The fipple may be the engine of the recorder, but the bore and fingerholes are the running gear and bodywork, and a well-tuned bore can turn a three-legged mutt into a race winning greyhound. It's like the difference between singing into a cathedral and singing into a sack of potatoes. A resonant space takes the sound and amplifies it and feeds back on itself so that as little as possible of that energy is lost.

The most resonant bore is a parallel tube with a loud fundamental, few partials; and a strong basic tone. How the early makers came up with the idea of tapering the bore we will never know; maybe someone bored a recorder from both ends with a blunt bayonet and never quite met in the middle giving the first choked bore by serendipity. However, once the idea of a tapered bore got around, makers started playing with the idea, and eventually came up with the baroque bore with its complex tapers that produce the characteristic rich sound and extended range of the high baroque originals. A tapered bore, by flattening the lower end of the range, also gives the opportunity to raise fingerholes to within easy reach, thus making larger recorders more feasible than with a parallel bore.

I should also mention that the contemporary recorder has returned to the open parallel bore, with its powerful lower notes, and persuaded it to work beyond the accepted baroque range using baroque fingering, but the subtlety of tone of the tapered bore remains far more suitable for the repertoire of the baroque period.

The fingerholes are spaced with two ideas in mind, that they should give the correct pitches, and also that they should be comfortable for the hands. On smaller recorders they can be spaced more equally, but as the recorder gets longer they have to be arranged in a closely-spaced left-hand and right-hand group. On the large renaissance originals these two groups are spaced apart from each other, and the tuning is controlled by the size of the fingerhole rather than the position, so you will see a large hole above a medium hole with a small hole underneath. If the hole position is too far for fingers to reach we see various combinations of keywork, and modern basses and great basses can be keyed throughout.

DIY Tuning is not as difficult as it sounds, but it must be followed in a logical and ordered manner. When I tune a recorder from scratch I follow a cyclical pattern, starting by tuning the recorder to about 20 cents below pitch, then re-voicing, and finishing and cleaning the bore. This will give the voicing a chance to work better, so the tone will be stronger, and then I can tune the recorder again and clean it up again. If you take a note in isolation and bring it up to pitch before finalising the voicing, you will inevitably find that it is sharp when the recorder is finished and the recorder is working at full power. A further complication is that the bore also contributes to the sound, and until the bore is right the tone will never develop fully.

Each hole will make a contribution to the pitch of several notes; with diminishing effect the further away you get from the first open hole. However, the higher harmonics are sometimes affected by unexpected holes, and not by others. You can do some experimentation yourself. Play a particular note into a tuning meter, and then cover each open fingerhole in turn and see what effect it has on the pitch. You will probably end up with results something like the following:

Finger hole terminology as applied to the following tables.

O- Left hand thumb closed,
   -Left hand thumb pinched
1- Left hand index finger
2- Left hand middle finger
3- Left hand ring finger
4- Right hand index finger
5- Right hand middle finger
6- Right hand ring finger, both holes covered
6Ø-Right hand ring finger, one hole covered
7- Right hand little finger, both holes covered
7Ø-Right hand little finger, one hole covered
8- End of foot joint.

Influence of tone hole adjustments on the tuning of a treble baroque recorder with single holes.

Note	Fingering	Remaining open holes in order of pitch influence
F	01234567	8
G	0123456	7 8
A	012345	6 7 8
B flat	0123467	5 8
B	012356	4 7 8
C	0123	4 5 6 7 8
C#	012456Ø	3 6 7 8
D	012	3 4 5 6 7 8
E flat	0134	2 5 6 7 8
E	01	2 3 4 5 6 7 8
F	02	1 3 4 5 6 7 8
F#	12	0 3 4 5 6 7 8
G	2	0 1 3 4 5 6 7 8
G#	23456	0 7 1 8
A	Ø12345	6 7 8
B flat	Ø12346	5 7 8
B nat.	Ø1235	4 6 7 8
C	Ø123	4 5 6 7 8
C#	Ø124	3 5 6 7 8
D	Ø12	3 4 5 6 7 8
E flat	Ø12456	7 8 3
E	Ø1245	6 7 8 3
F	Ø145	2 6 7 8 3

The bore also affects the tuning, and once again you can experiment by adding material to the bore in different places and seeing what effect it has. A dynamic way to try this effect is to mount a piece of material, wax, plasticine or some such, on a length of wire that is fixed to the bench, and then move the recorder on to it so that it can travel up and down the bore while playing the same note into a tuning meter.

You will see the pitch rise and fall as the 'constriction' passes various key points, and these will be different for each note. This means that any note can be tuned individually using the bore in conjunction with the fingerholes, but the bore is most often used for tuning octaves where the same fingering has to give two notes that are exactly one octave apart. In a parallel bore this happens via simple physics-halving the length of the tube doubles the frequency of the note – but in a tapered bore you have to be more cunning. For example, the octave A on an alto can be tuned by opening the bore between holes 1 and 2. If the bore is too small at this point the octave will be narrow. As the bore is opened the lower A falls in pitch and the upper A rises until they sound a precise octave. At that point hole 6 can be opened up and the pitch of both will rise together until it is correct. When the bore is right, the lower A will also develop a harmonic allowing it to be blown more strongly, and the high E natural, [the harmonic twelfth of A] which is also controlled largely by the same hole 6 as the two As, will also be better in tune.

The effect of adding material to the bore can be seen in Fig. 21 [Many thanks to Adrian Brown for allowing me to adapt his original artwork.] These measurements were taken using an air blower so that the pressure could be kept constant, but you will still see the same effects using your lungs. As adding material to the bore effects notes in a particular way, the logical extension to this is that removing material from the bore will have the opposite effect. Have a play with the bore using paper strips or wax or some plastic cut from a curved bottle to add material. For removing material, you really need adjustment reamers, which are covered in the next section.

Tuning with the Bore and Fingerholes

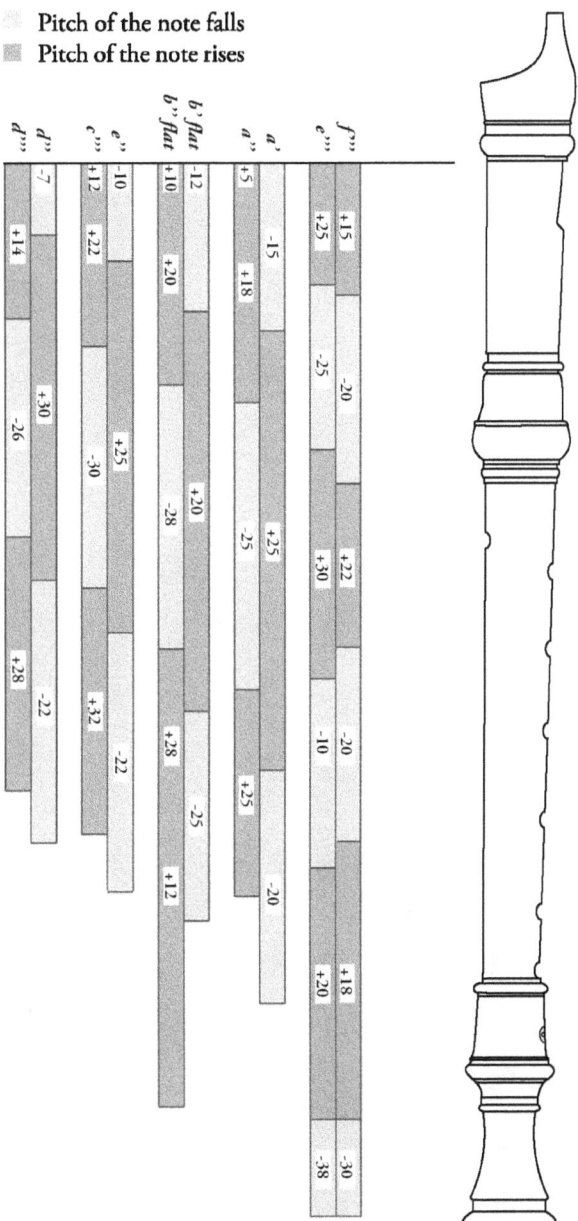

The effect of bore diameter changes in a baroque treble recorder.
Numbers denote position and maximum pitch change
observed when an object of consistent size is passed along the bore.
Many thanks to Adrian brown for permission to adapt his original artwork.

Fig. 21 [to be associated with the above]

Obedience Training for Recorders - *Tim Cranmore*

Bore Profiles. All makers worked at some time from bore diagrams taken from original recorders, and they will give you a good idea of how the early makers operated. A typical baroque bore diagram is given in figure 22

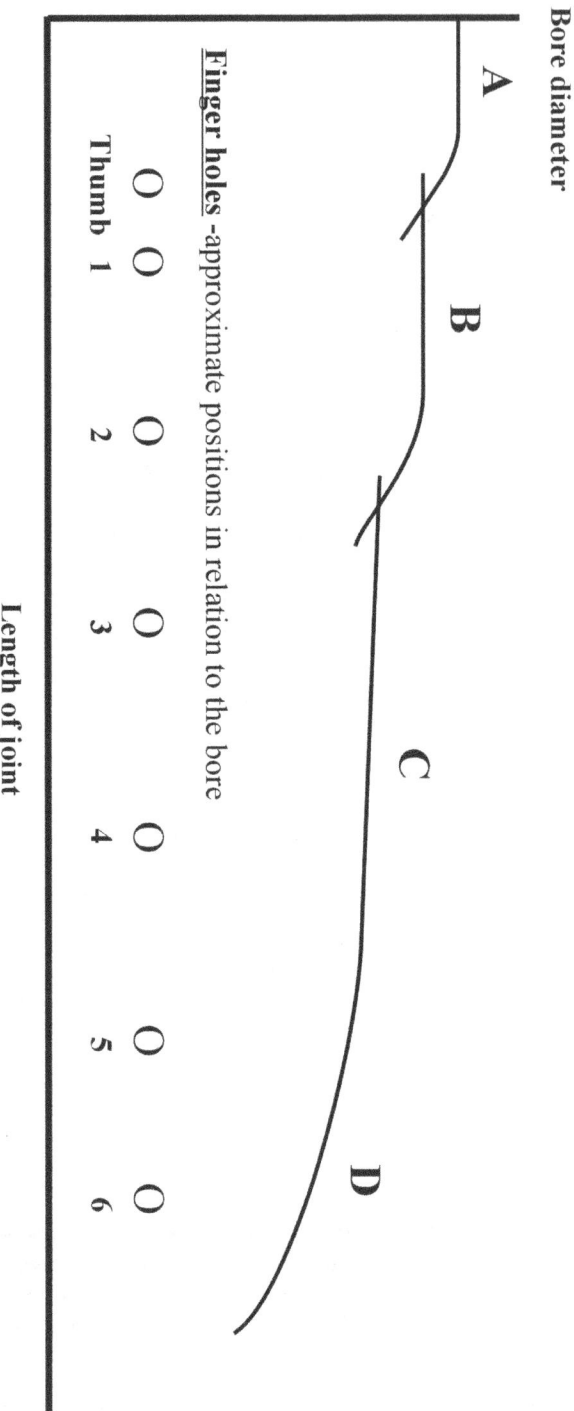

This diagram shows a typical centre joint bore profile for a baroque recorder, a view that appears time and time again when examining original instruments of all sizes. There are four distinct zones, each of which bears on the performance of the recorder. These are, for an alto recorder;

Zone A - A section of enlargement within the top joint which contributes towards the octave of D
Zone B - A section of enlargement between holes 2 and 3 which contributes to the tuning of A and high E
Zone C - A largely parallel section with little useful tuning potential leading to;
Zone D - an enlarged section which can be used to tune high E and which joins to the foot bore.

Fig. 22 Schematic diagram of a baroque recorder centre joint bore

As you can see, the taper is not straight, but has separate sections, some of which appear to be parallel, and some taper sharply. I soon realised that this is the effect of using several reamers to adjust the bore, and familiarity with this technique can make all the difference during the final stages of adjustment. I have also designed completely new instruments using this basic template, and an instinctive idea of what the new dimensions need to be. The entire lower bore derives from the head joint diameter, and once you have decided on that, the rest follows.

You can make your own bore diagrams using several techniques. Some very elaborate machinery has been designed using sprung-caliper measuring instruments fitted with strain gauges, but I believe that the simplest way is best. You can buy measuring gauges that are a simple spring-loaded mechanism, which opens to the diameter of the bore, and can then be locked into position before being withdrawn from the recorder. By measuring the depth that a particular gauge has reached at a particular diameter, the bore diagram can be drawn by plotting diameter against depth. An alternative method, which I used myself, is to turn a series of nylon discs at 0.2mm diameter increments. These can be mounted one by one on a measuring rod and used in the same way as the adjustable gauges.

Reaming the Bore.

A lot of hot air has been expended on the subject of reamers and bores. Basically, what works, works and whether a bore has been made to a tolerance of 1/100mm with a beautifully hardened, tempered and ground, fluted reamer or with a bit of wood fitted with a scraping blade makes no difference. It is the balanced whole that matters made with the tools that the maker is accustomed to. I have seen a velvet-lined drawer containing spotless steel reamers, and mine live in a plastic cutlery container, and are largely made out of oak and bandsaw blade. They can produce a beautiful, long shaving, instead of a pile of wood dust, and can be made in minutes and easily discarded if faulty. Having said that, some of mine have been in use now for 20 years or more The final reaming of a recorder is not a question of reaching pre-determined parameters, but of listening to the instrument and knowing just which reamer of several to use to give it the final tweak. Engineers tend to start by producing one-piece reamers, which exactly copy the bore of the original they are working from, and can never quite understand why they usually don't work.

Making a Simple Wooden Adjustment Reamer.

Assuming you have a lathe and some skill with it, find a piece of oak or similar hardwood, long enough to reach just beyond the point of the bore that you want to experiment with, plus 5cm for a handle [Fig. 23].

Take a diameter from the bore diagram <u>below</u> the point you are interested in, and knock off a millimetre for clearance, and decide what diameter you want to expand the bore to. Use these as your maximum and minimum. Turn the wood to these sizes minus 0.5mm plus a short parallel section, giving a cutting length of about 4-5cm to adjust a treble, and then back off from the maximum to make the handle. Saw along the reaming section leaving a slightly fat D-shaped cross-section, and then take a length of band saw blade, grind off the teeth, and drill and screw it to the wood, with one edge standing about 1mm above the round surface, and the other safely below it, so that it will eventually cut when rotating clockwise. [I find that an old band saw blade that has done many thousand revolutions is sufficiently soft to be drillable, but still takes a good edge. In other words, ask your local woodworking shop for a broken one – don't try to hacksaw it, you can break it to length by clamping it in the vice and then bending it backwards and forwards.]

Grind the cutting edge tangentially to the reamer surface until the maximum and minimum diameters are the ones you are after, with the maximum extended into the parallel section, and try it out. Always clean and oil the bore after reaming to get the best tone, and polish and oil thoroughly when you are satisfied.

If engineering is more your forte, a length of silver steel can be turned to the required profile, and then milled and ground to give a D-shaped cross-section as seen in fig. 24.

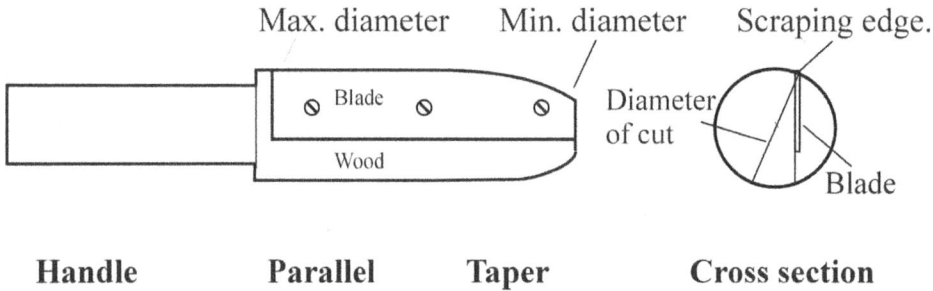

Fig. 23

– A simple wooden adjustment reamer.

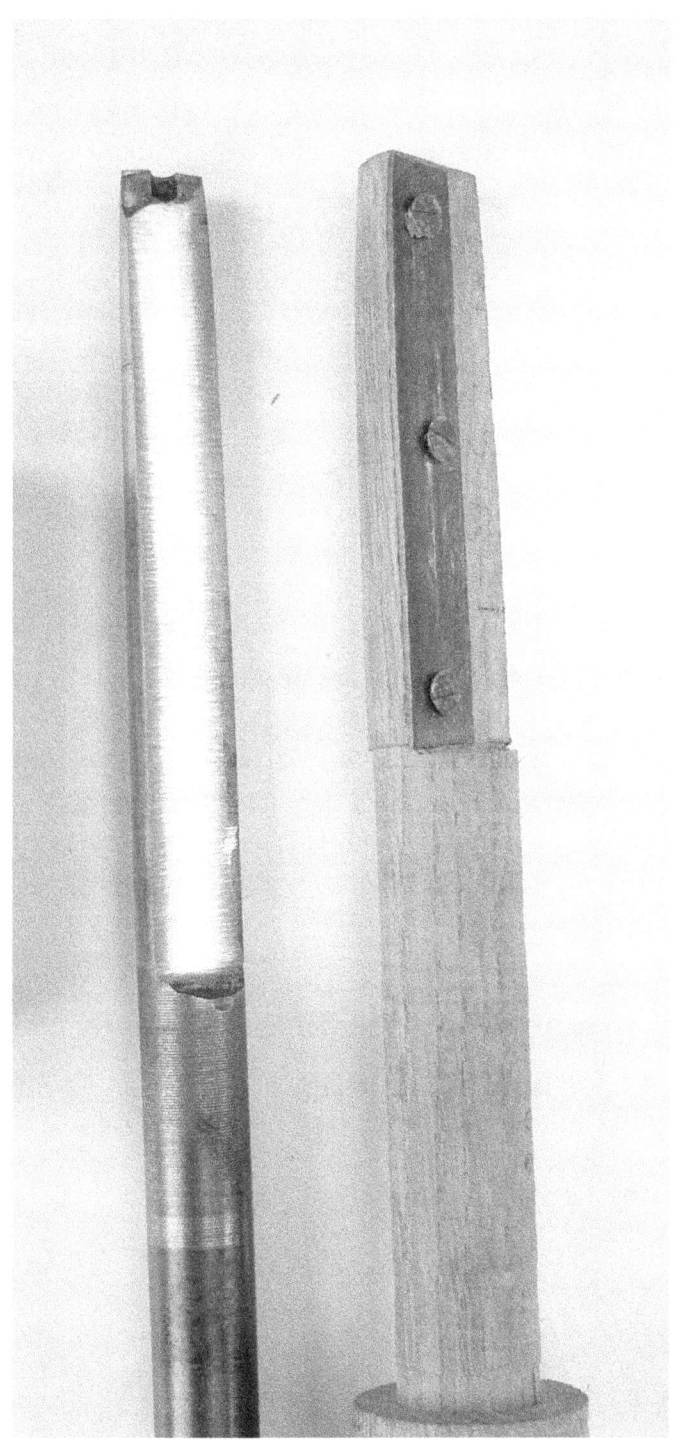

Fig. 24 – Steel and wooden reamers.

Obedience Training for Recorders - *Tim Cranmore*

Tuning, step by step.

Overall, a simple rule is start from the bottom, and head for the top, but first you have to ask some questions of the recorder as a whole.

1. Is the recorder overall too flat? Rather than attempt to adjust each note, try drilling a small hole of 1mm diameter in the side of the head joint just by the window. This should raise the pitch overall. If insufficiently, drill two. You can always block them up if the room gets warmer.
2. Is the recorder too sharp? Pulling out is, of course, an answer, but can give problems with the octaves as a space is formed between the head and the centre. Get a washer made up to fill this space, or try building up the outside wall around the window with some wax or similar material as an alternative.
3. To use a treble recorder as an example, is the octave A too large, or have the low C or D got a strange hollow sound when pushed, with a high top octave? Or conversely, are these octaves too small with a weak low note and a flat top octave? If so then the bore may be incorrect, and this should be seen to before any changes are made to fingerholes. These adjustments are treated in the following table.

Tuning table.

Techniques referred to in this table include filling holes, opening holes and bore adjustment [method given above.]. For opening holes, use a needle file, or a small, sharp blade. For closing holes, run superglue into the wall of the hole and let it dry, or melt beeswax into it using a hot scalpel blade or wire. For bore adjustments, material can be reamed out [irreversible!], or replaced temporarily with wax, rolled card, or a section cut from a plastic bottle, or more permanently with epoxy resin or two part-varnish. Epoxy can be reamed to a new profile when properly set, and is hardly detectible on first sight.

All processes apply to a treble recorder in F, but equally transfer to any size. See table on page 44 for hole descriptions.

Low F. Largely controlled by hole 8. Insert wax etc. to flatten, ream out to sharpen, but bear in mind the effect on the highest notes.

Low F#. Controlled by hole 7Ø. Enlarge to sharpen, fill to flatten.

Low G. Controlled by hole 7. Enlarge to sharpen, fill to flatten.

Low G# /A flat Controlled by hole 6Ø. Enlarge to sharpen, fill to flatten.

Tuning with the Bore and Fingerholes

Low A. Controlled by hole 6. Enlarge to sharpen, fill to flatten, but bear in mind that this octave is very inflexible unless the bore is correct, and enlarging hole 6 [and hole 7] will raise both high E and high F. Also controlled by the bore between holes 1 and 2. Open to widen the octave, close to narrow the octave.

! ALL THE PRECEDING CAN ALTER THE HIGH REGISTER FROM E UPWARDS – check as you go along!

Low B flat. Sharpen by undercutting hole 5 to the north; flatten by filling in on north side.

Low B natural. Sharpen by undercutting hole 4 to the north. This will preferentially sharpen B nat. in relation to low C, but bear in mind that a very sharp B nat. with an 'in tune' low C is difficult to correct, and an alternative fingering should be looked for. Flatten in the opposite way but with the same provisos.

Low C. Sharpen by undercutting hole 4 to the north, but bear in mind that this will preferentially sharpen low B nat., and this note may need an alternative fingering. If the low C is flat compared to high C, and has a 'boomy' tone, try filling in the bore opposite the thumbhole.

Low C#. This is best adjusted using alternative fingerings, as changing hole 3 affects several other notes.

Low D. Sharpen by undercutting hole 3 to the north, flatten by filling. If low D is flat compared to high D, and has a rasping sound, try filling in the bore above the thumbhole.

Low E flat. Sharpen by enlarging hole 2 to the south. This will also raise high F, so consider alternative fingerings.

Low E. Sharpen by undercutting hole 2 to the north, and flatten by filling.

Middle F. Sharpen by undercutting hole 1 to the north, and flatten by filling, but remember that this hole also affects middle G.

Middle F#. Sharpen by undercutting thumbhole to the south, and flatten by filling.

Middle G. Sharpen by undercutting thumbhole to the north, and flatten by filling.

Middle G# using OO234560. Sharpen by undercutting hole 1 to the south, and flatten by filling, but this is a difficult note to change.

Obedience Training for Recorders - *Tim Cranmore*

Middle G# using ∅123456∅. Tune with 6∅ but always in conjunction with low G#

!WHILE ADJUSTING TUNING ALWAYS LISTEN TO OTHER NOTES THAT MIGHT BE AFFECTED BY THE SAME HOLES - and don't go too far at once!

High A. Sharpen by undercutting or enlarging hole 6 to the south, or flatten by filling, but bear in mind that this octave is very inflexible unless the bore is correct, and enlarging hole 6 will raise both high E and high F. Also controlled by the bore between holes 1 and 2. Open to widen the octave, close to narrow the octave.

High B flat. Sharpen by undercutting or enlarging hole 5 to the south. Flatten by filling.

High B nat. Sharpen by undercutting hole 4 to the south. This note will be preferentially sharpened over high C. Flatten by filling.

High C. Sharpen by undercutting hole 4 to the south, flatten by filling, but keep an ear on high B nat. If the octave is too wide, flatten high C by reducing the bore opposite the thumbhole.

High C#. Sharpen by undercutting hole 3 and/or hole 5 to the south if you have a slightly flat B flat. Flatten by filling, but keep an ear on high D nat.

High D. Sharpen by undercutting hole 3 to the south, flatten by filling but keep an ear on C#. This note is best adjusted in the bore. Addition of material just in the top joint will narrow the octave, and removal of material will widen it, but keep an ear on the tone, as too wide an octave will result in an unpleasant hollow tone to most of the middle range.

High E flat. This note is often so tied up with the other top range that the best way to cope with poor tuning is to find alternative fingerings by adding right hand fingers.

High E nat. This note is controlled by both the open right hand holes including the end of the bore, but mainly hole 6, which is why it is so tied up with A. It is often too high, and you can adjust the bore by reaming around the end of the centre and top of the foot joint, or use a combination of hole 6 and 7 if you want to try filling. As mentioned before, adjusting the bore between holes 1 and 2 can bring the A octave and high E into harmony with each other.

High F nat. This note is controlled by the holes at the end of the recorder similar to High E, but with the added advantage that hole 2 also affects the pitch. There may be some conflict with the low E flat, but making hole 2 larger to the south or filling it, will either sharpen or flatten respectively.

High G. A difficult note whose pitch is largely subject to the pitch of everything else. Most players are happy to adjust the pitch by covering hole 7 to a varying degree, and quite honestly, that is what I usually tell them to do.

Don't forget the Golden Rule – treat the recorder as a whole. Correction of voicing and tuning must go hand in hand. Cleanliness is everything. Eventually you will get a feel for the complete instrument and realise that it is far more than the sum of its parts – just like man's best friend!

Obedience Training for Recorders - *Tim Cranmore*

CHAPTER 6

Miscellaneous

Fruit, n 'veg.

There are apparently two bodies of people who have a great interest in straightening the banana. One is the EEC fruit and vegetable trading standards department, the other is composed entirely of recorder makers. However, while the former wrestle with the problem of standardising bent yellow fruit, I can announce that after much research, [actually, one or two traumatic attempts!], I have cracked the problem of straightening bent yellow recorder joints.

One of the most common consequences of mixing modern central heating and boxwood recorders is the banana-shaped centre joint. This is caused by poor seasoning, and uneven drying of the wood after it has been turned, and although a small deviation is no particular problem, a positive bend can be, especially if it is to the left and against the natural shape of the hand. If you really can't live with it, a banana-shaped boxwood centre joint can be straightened by the application of heat. For a treble recorder, put your centre joint in the microwave for absolutely no more than 30 seconds [high power from cold in my 600watt oven], and then gently but quickly clamp the joint between two supports as shown with a slight bend in the opposite direction to the curvature. After a few hours the joint, with luck, will be set straight.

Fig. 25 – Straightening a bent centre joint.

On a similar topic, there is a recent vogue for constructing recorders out of carrots. I have to say that I dismissed this as a passing food fad, but when I tried it myself, it actually worked and made a very appetising sound. There are various videos of these on the Internet, and I can recommend the Vienna Vegetable Orchestra as a source of recipes. It also crossed my mind that making carrot recorders is a very environmentally friendly way of getting to understand basic voicing without taking too much time per instrument, and using very cheap raw materials. They don't last for very long, but when you get one to work it will play for a day or two, and can then be re-cycled as a wholesome addition to supper. [See back cover].

Coda.

Straightening a centre joint in the microwave possibly requires the greatest leap of faith that I have yet asked you to make, which is why it is at the end of the book. Besides it all other leaps seem insignificant. This is the one from a great height without the parachute, and I can't guarantee a soft landing for this, or any other of the outrageous suggestions that pepper this book. All I can say is that it all works for me, but then I've been mad enough to be a recorder trainer for 30 years and my graduates are in regular use all round the world. It is possible that if you follow my well-intentioned, if occasionally slightly disturbing, advice, you may well end up with a piece of firewood, [the way the flames come out of the fingerholes is particularly attractive], but you may also be the proud owner of the best-behaved recorder in polite society, well enough behaved to be let off its lead, play nicely with the other recorders without biting, and even show them up by its discipline, tone, and general harmony with the rest of the group. You will be the envy of all your friends, who will no doubt want to copy your training techniques for themselves. Please feel free to direct them to their nearest bookshop.

Being a Recorder-Maker.

I sort of just fell into recorder-making. I had completely forgotten that I had tried to make a descant recorder at school from the branch of a crab apple tree in my parent's garden [I found it later – it never had a chance of working!], but when I found myself unemployed and on a bit of a pub crawl with my recorder teacher, it seemed like a remarkably good idea to try making recorders.

He had just taken delivery of his brand new, A410, Andreas Glatt, Stanesby copy, which I was only allowed to look at gleaming in its box, and he insisted that the world needed recorder makers! – England needed recorder makers!!, and it was my patriotic duty to immediately take up the challenge. Besides, he knew a man who knew everything there was to know about the subject [he didn't!!], and money would fall out of the skies as soon as I produced England's first historically accurate copies of the great makers' instruments!! [It didn't do that either-or at least not for a while].

Anyway, I moved from a clinical laboratory on the 13th floor of Guy's Hospital, to a former chicken shed near Oxford, sat myself in a corner, and tried to work it out. This was my first mistake. I should have travelled, measured, networked, advertised, asked questions – but instead, dear reader, I sat in a corner and tried to work it out! My nadir was the reaction of the Craft Council when I applied for money. Apparently I was only a reproducer of antiques of particular interest, so didn't deserve any.

However, if there is one quality that I, and any potential maker, must possess, it is perseverance, and when I finally produced something worth playing, the world seemed very interested indeed.

The first time I sold a recorder I had a party! [I had to pay him back because it was no good, but I don't usually mention that]. I gradually discovered travelling – Europe, the States, the whole recorder world, and despite my inauspicious start, the business soon began generating enough money to support a young family.

My colleagues, all young and ambitious, were in the same position as me, and I soon realised that I was in a very small working community that was scattered all over the world. Thirty years on, the faces are largely the same, although the hair is greyer.

At the time of writing the market is a bit overcrowded and I could not wholeheartedly recommend giving up the day job to make recorders, but it is a very good time to be thinking about it, as there are very few young people in what is still a strong body of experienced makers, and numbers will start dropping off as the hand of mortality casts its long shadow.

So my advice is travel, measure, network, ask questions, but wait until you have produced work that has been checked over by a couple of friendly professionals first before you think of exhibiting, and choose ones that will tell you the truth, not just be polite. First impressions will last for years!

As one of the many makers who started in the late 1970's I can confirm that we were a pretty competitive lot, and I have many memories of recorder festivals, the cutting edge of the free market. Imagine the scene – that rare beast, a paying customer, walks into an echoing hall lined with an international assembly of recorder makers – he takes one from each and leaves the room – 30 minutes later he is back and slowly walks from one to the other and returns their instrument – the tension mounts – who will be the last, the winner! – down to three, two, and then we all know. The winning maker puts on a barely suppressed smile of triumph, writes off his mortgage for that month, and everyone else pretends that it doesn't really matter and glares into their lap.

I have been to shows the far side of Europe where not one recorder player has appeared and we have all gone to the nearest bar and packed up early. Conversely, I have also known occasions where my case has been emptied by frantic students the moment I opened it, and I made half a year's income in a day and spent the rest of the show with an empty table, a silly smile on my face and a pocket full of cheques. Next year I have watched exactly the same happen to the maker next door! It is truly a free market!

Ps. People will think you are very strange, but smile at them as you commute to your workshop at the bottom of the garden, take the dog for a walk, or just stay in bed all day.

Festivals.

The major European exhibitions are a marvellous place to get an impression of the commercial side of the recorder. Most of them have been going for years, so I would safely assume that they would still be there for some time after this book is in print.

They are;

January –Resonanzen Ancient Music Festival in Vienna – www.konzerthaus.at

April – Musicora in Paris- *www.musicora.net*

May – Stockstadt Alte Muziktage near Frankfurt- www.stockstaedter-musiktage.de

June – Boston Early Music Festival - www.bemf.org

August –Flanders Festival in Brugge [every three years] - www.musica-antiqua.com

September – Utrecht - www.oudemuziek.nl

October –Berliner Tage fur Alte Musik - www.berlinaltemusik.com

November – London Early Music Exhibition - www.earlymusicshop.com

There are other exhibitions in various parts of the world, but these are the big players for my money! Go for a visit first – Stockstadt is probably the most interesting – and network furiously! It will pay off.

Measurements

I used the excellent series of drawings by Fred Morgan of the Bruggen collection, published by Zen-On, which I believe is out of print, but occasionally surfaces for sale second hand. Adrian Brown's book of measurements of the Vienna collection is available via his website, and Jan Bouterse has published a comprehensive volume of measurements of Dutch instruments. Often, the museums where instruments are held will have plans available. The Bate Collection in Oxford, for example, has plans of its excellent Bressan alto and others.

Current Active Individual-Recorder Makers.

Here follows a list of active makers of hand –made instruments, largely taken from Nick Lander's excellent website http://www.recorderhomepage.net which is in itself a wonderful source of information. Some were kind enough to send a short note about themselves, which I have reproduced here. I have only included workshops that are associated with a single, named maker, who knows the process from beginning to end. Other workshops such as Moeck, Mollenhauer, Dolmetsch, Takeyama, Fehr and Coolsma produce high quality instruments but they are less individually made than those listed below.

Contact;
Joel Arpin,
104, rue de Moulignon,   Tel; 0033 1 60 04 82 71
F - 77860 Quincy-Voisins   Email; *joel.arpin@free.fr*
France   Website; *http://joel.arpin.free.fr/*

Ragnar Arvidsson - was an engineer and musician, and played the recorder since he was a teenager, in a series of different ensembles through the years. Because he was technically-minded he soon started to try to adjust, and then make his own instruments. In the summer of 1985 he attended a recorder-making course in Austria, taught by Alec Loretto. It was there that he found the solutions to many of the remaining problems. The first recorders he made for customers were delivered in 1988. Since then recorders he has made have ended up all over the map from Piteå (in the very north of Sweden) to Barcelona.

Based on some mathematical relations, familiar from his engineering work, he succeeded in designing a new baroque recorder bore. This bore is the result of a straightforward design process and can be completely described by a mathematical equation. The instruments built with this new bore have a very stable and full tone in the low end of the range and a fast attack and good equality over the whole range.

Contact;
Ragnar Arvidsson,
Tättingegatan 6,   Tel; 00 46 3129 7442
S 426 69 V. Frölunda,   Email; *ragnara@telia.com*
Sweden.   Website; *http://www.recorder-arvidsson.se/*

Vincent Bernolin - followed in the footsteps of his father, Roger Bernolin, who was Professor of Recorder at the Conservatoire superieure of Geneva for 30 years, and who made several recorders for himself. Vincent trained at the conservatoire as a pianist, but on graduating in 1994, decided to pursue a career as a maker of both recorders and granadilla Boehm style modern flutes. In 2006 he won the prize for the best musical instrument maker in France from the French Ministry of Culture. His instruments include baroque recorders from soprano to voice flute, Ganassi and van Eyck pre-baroque instruments, and a Rafi consort.

Contact;
Vincent Bernolin,
12, Rue de la Plaine,
34120 Castelnau de Guers,
France.

Phone 0033 [0]467359780
E-mail *vincent@bernolin.fr*
Website *www.bernolin.fr*

Contact;
Stephan Blezinger,
Meisterwerkstätte für Flötenbau
Schillerstraße 11
D-99817 Eisenach

Phone 0049(0)3691-212346
Fax 0049(0)3691-212348
Email; *info@blezinger.de*
Website; *http://www.blezinger.de/*

Phillipe Bolton

Contact;
Le Grand Portail,
84570 Villes sur Auzon
France.

Tel; 0033 4 90 61 86 11
Email; *philippe_bolton@flute-a-bec.com*
Website; *http://www.flute-a-bec.com/*

Jan Bouterse - studied ecology and nature conservation at the Wageningen University before he became interested in making copies of recorders and traversos. His investigation involved the examination of historical instruments. In 2001, he received a doctorate in musicology from the Utrecht University (2001). In 2005, a revised and updated version of the dissertation (Dutch woodwind instruments and their makers, 1660 - 1760) was published by the KVNM (Koninklijke Vereniging voor Nederlandse Muziekgesc hiedenis): Jan Bouterse co-authored the three catalogues of Dutch baroque woodwind instruments in the Gemeentemuseum at The Hague and has written articles for the Bouwbrief, the Journal of the American Musical Instrument Society, Tibia and the FoMRHI-Quarterly. He is still active in making and repairing woodwind instruments and giving workshops, and writes articles not only about musical instruments but also about nature conservation and wildlife management.

Contact;
Jan Bouterse,
Sandenburg 29,
2402 Rj Alphen, A/D Rijn
Holland.

Tel; 0031 [0]172 445957
Email; *mcjbouterse@freeler.nl*
Website; *http://home.hetnet.nl/~mcjbouterse/*

Current Active Individual Recorder Makers.

Adriana Breukink started playing the recorder at the age of nine. When she was sixteen she went to the Conservatory in Rotterdam, and three years later to the Royal Conservatory at The Hague. There she studied recorder with Ricardo Kanji and Frans Brüggen. During her last year she took a course with Fred Morgan in making recorders, in the Conservatory workshop. In 1980 she completed her Solo exam in recorder, and then she opened her own workshop for making recorders. For many years she has been known for making Renaissance Consorts, Ganassi recorders and Dream recorders, and her customers include soloists, ensembles and conservatories all over the world. In recent years, she has developed many new instruments, such as the Slide Recorder for Moeck, and the Dream Soprano, -Alto, -Tenor and -Bass for Mollenhauer. One of her recent recorders is the 3 metre (10 foot) long Sub-contrabass in Bb. Her latest project is to develop a new concept about breathing types to help in adapting the right windway position to the blowing style of the player.

Contact;
Adriana Breukink,
Nieuwe Schoolweg 28,
NL-7514 CG Enschede   Email; *info@adrianabreukink.com*
Holland.   Website; *http://www.adrianabreukink.com/*

Contact;
Adrian Brown,
Delistraat 44 / Postbus 2595,   Tel; 0031 64811 5476
NL-1000 CN, Amsterdam,   Email; *flutes@adrianbrown.org*
Holland.   Website; *http://www.adrianbrown.org/*

David Coomber-Klitgaard - has been making recorders for 22 years. He started making in Holland while studying recorder at the Royal Conservatorium in the Hague, and the Stedelijk Conservatorium in Zwolle. Frederick Morgan gave several classes in recorder making at the Royal Conservatorium while he was in Europe in 1978. One of David Coomber's greatest assets as a maker is his experience as a player and performer. He teaches the recorder to postgraduate level at Auckland University's School of Music. David's philosophy is to make the best quality recorders and that no recorder leaves the workshop unless it is up to the standards demanded of a professional instrument. David is always prepared to work alongside musicians to ensure the recorder they purchase meets their demands.

Contact;
David Coomber-Klitgaard,   Tel; 0064 98377903
PO Box 12-1165,   Fax; 0064 98376144
Henderson, Auckland 8,   Email; Hawkridge@xtra.co.nz
New Zealand.   Website; http://www.coomber-fern-recorders.co.nz

Contact;
Tim Cranmore,
23, Lower Chase Rd.
Malvern,
Worcs. WR14 2BX
U.K.

Tel; 00441684 563313
Email; *tc@fippleflute.co.uk*
Website; *http://www.fippleflute.co.uk*

Contact;
Bodil Diesen,
Greverudåsen 14,
1415 Oppegaard,
Norway.

Tel; 0047 2 994805
Email; *post@bodildiesen.no*
Website; *http://www.bodildiesen.no/*

Contact;
Marc Ecochard,
Tonne, Cidex 32,
16430 Vindelle,
France.

Tel; 0033 5 45 21 49 18
Email; *marc.ecochard@grandhautbois-flutes.com*
Website; *http://marc.ecochard.free.fr/*

Contact;
Ralf Ehlert
Gartenkamp 6,
Celle/Bostel
Germany.

Tel; 00 49 5141 930181
Email; *info@ehlert-blockfloeten.de*
Website; *http://www.ehlert-blockfloeten.de/*

Contact;
Andreas Glatt,
Eikstraat 31,
B-1673 Beert,
Belgium.

Tel; 0032 2 356 18 78
Email; *info@andreasglatt.be*
Website; *http://www.andreasglatt.be/*

Contact;
Henri Gohin,
16 rue Macaigne Fortier,
F-95650 Boissy l'Aillerie,
France.

Tel; 00 33 1 34 66 91 26
Email; *henri.gohin@free.fr*

Current Active Individual Recorder Makers.

Contact;
Michael Grinter,
'Snug', Elmtree Lane,
Chewton Vic. 3451,
Australia.

Tel; 00 61 3 5472-3990
Email; *grinter@castlemaine.net.au*
Website; *http://www.grinterflutes.com/*

Contact;
Marcelo D. Gurovich,
Sarmiento 3725 4°,
Argentina.

Email; *marcelogu2000@yahoo.com*
Website; *http://www.mg-woodwinds.com.ar/*

Contact;
Jan Hermans
Historical Woodwinds
Braambeslei 11
2950 KAPELLEN

Tel./fax: 00-32-3/666 89 33
Email; *jan.hermans@historicalwoodwinds.be*
Website; *http://www.historicalwoodwinds.be/*

Von Huene Recorders. - Friedrich von Huene has been a pioneer in the reproduction of historical woodwinds for nearly half a century. Born and raised in Germany, he emigrated to the US in 1948. He began making recorders in 1960 and was awarded a Guggenheim Fellowship in 1966 for a comparative study of historical woodwinds. He designed the Rottenburgh model for Moeck, and the first high-quality plastic recorders for Zen-On. After a successful career as a professional chef, Patrick von Huene joined the workshop as an apprentice in 1982, and for nearly 20 years he has overseen production. When not carving recorders, he enjoys exotic automobiles, fine cooking and jazz.

Von Huene Workshop, Inc.
65 Boylston St.
Brookline, MA 02445
USA

Tel; 001 617 277-8690
Fax; 001 617 277-7217
Email; *info@vonhuene.com*
Website; *http://www.vonhuene.com/*

Contact;
Shigeharu Hirao,
7-10-11-Nakagawa,
Kohoku-ku,
Yokohoma-shi,
Kanagawa, Japan.

Tel; 045 913 1184
Email; *s-hirao@yk.rim.or.jp*

Etienne Holmblat - Studied the flute for ten years, and became increasingly interested in the baroque repertoire, especially that for the recorder. He made his first recorder in 1982, an alto after J Heitz, and followed that with instruments after Bressan, Stanesby, Denner, Terton, and most recently an alto after Rafi

Contact;
Etienne Holmblat,
31, Route du Pietat, Tel; 0033 872 988 009
64290 Bosdarros, Email; *etienne.holmblat@wanadoo.fr*
France. Website; *http://www.holmblat.fr/*

Guido and Marie Hulsens Guido Hulsens makes :renaissance consort after instruments in Brussels and Vienna. Ganassi recorders ; Rafi recorders ; Baroque instruments after originals from Stanesby, Bressan, Denner, Steenbergen, Reich. Csakan after Ziegler. Also student instruments.

Contact;
Guido Hulsens,
Beaubourg, Tel; 0033 05 4594 0951
F-16330 Coulonge, Email; *hulsens@aol.com*
France. Website; *http://guido.hulsens.free.fr/*

Guido Maria Klemisch – Studied with Frans Brüggen at the Royal Conservatory of The Hague (The Netherlands), where he graduated in 1973. At the end of his studies he learnt wood-wind making with Klaus Scheele (Germany) and attended the organology class of Bruce Haynes at The Hague. In 1974 he started his own work-shop and built up his career as recorder/ flute-player and baroque oboist with the Camerata Amsterdam. Since 2002 he has designed and built several renaissance recorder consorts based on HIER.S, SCHNITZER, BASSANO and VALIANI, and in 1998 he moved with his family to Berlin (Germany) working there since then, and in 2005 he founded the KLEMISCH-CONSORT BERLIN playing 15th, 16th and early 17th-century music on his own accurate and authentic copies of instruments from the period.

Contact;
Guido Maria Klemisch
Frithjofstr. 71 Tel: 0049 30 47307098
D – 13089 Berlin, Email: info@guido-m-klemisch.de
Germany Web-site: *www.guido-m-klemisch.de*

Current Active Individual Recorder Makers.

Eugene Ilarionov - graduated from the Mathematics Department of Kiev University in 1980 and was employed at the scientific institute of the same university. Early music was his favourite hobby, and in the 1990's, he played recorder and lute with two professional Ukrainian ensembles, "Greensleeves" and "Artes Liberales". He made his first instruments in 1990, and recorder making has been his only profession since 1999. Innovations from his workshop include medieval recorders, tabor pipes and the 'Rosenborg' recorder.

Contact;
Email; *fontegara@mail.ru*
Website; *http://www.fontegara.narod.ru*

Kobliczek Instrumentenbau GmbH / Christoph Hamman

Contact;	Tel; 0049 6128 734 03
Christoph Hamman,	Fax; 0049 6128 75181
Georg-Ohm-Str 14,	Email; *christoph.hammann@team-hammann.de*
6523 Taunusstein (Neuhof),	Website; *http://www.team-hammann.de/*
Germany.	

Heinrich and Maria Köllner-Dives - Began making recorders in 1983. Maria studied recorder in Vienna and received a concert diploma in 1976. Heinrich was a Catholic priest during 19 years and lost his profession by the marriage. At that time recorders were dear, and so they started to make the recorders themselves. They visited many workshops (for example Ulrich Hoehne, Bad Salzufflen, Paul Hailperin, Zell) and several times recorder makers of other workshops stayed with them at first in Landsut and since 1993 in Ludwigstal, including Alec Loretto.. They are building recorders of almost all periods: baroque, early baroque, Ganassi, etc. Their specialities are the medieval recorders (for example Dordrecht) and three hole pipes.

Contact;
Heinrich and Maria Köllner-Dives,

Bahnhofstrasse 5,	Tel; 0049 9925 1280
94227 Lindberg'	Email; *heinrich@koellnerdives.de*
Germany.	Website; *http://www.koellnerdives.de/*

Contact;
Doris Kulossa,
Wasserstr. 96 a,
D-44803 Bochum,
Germany.

Tel; 0049 234 3 61 60 62
Email; *doriskulossa@t-online.de*

Francesco Li Virghi - started to make recorders in 1980 because he was dissatisfied with those available in Italy at the time. Significant milestones were making a ceramic recorder together with Marco Piga in 1994, making the first Rafi recorder working with the historical J.deFer fingering in 1995, cylindricalrecorders in C and G in the VanEyck style, and in 2003 designing a five holed recorder with a range of one octave and half to use as a double recorder.

Contact;
Francesco Li Virghi
La Quercia del vento,
01028 Orte (VT),
Italy.

Tel; 00 39 761 402436
Email; *livirghi@tiscali.it*

Contact;
Margaret Löbner,
Osterdeich 59a,
D-28203 Bremen,
Germany.

Tel; 00 49 421 70 28 52
Email; *info@loebnerblockfloeten.de*
Website; *http://www.loebnerblockfloeten.de/ehome.htm*

Contact;
Albert Lockwood,
25 St Oswald Road,
Bridlington,
N Humberside YO 16 5SD

Email; *albert.lockwood@btinternet.com*
Website; *http://www.recorderhomepage.net/lockwood.html*

Bob Marvin – one of the founding fathers of modern recorder making, Bob has devoted himself to the production of renaissance consorts which exactly match the Italian originals. His consorts became available at the beginning of the early music revival, and were soon in use all round the world, with a legendary waiting list. Living a self-sufficient life near the USA/Canadian border, Bob still travels widely and welcomes contact from anyone with an interesting point of view.

Current Active Individual Recorder Makers.

Contact;
Bob Marvin,
Box 129 Eustis,
ME 04936, USA   Tel; 01 819 544 2091

Contact;
Ernst Meyer,
28, rue Kléber
F-93100 Montreuil,   Tel; 0033 6 795 791 30
France.   Email; meyerrecorders@mac.com

Contact;
Monika Musch
Sickingenstr. 10a   Tel; 0049 761 456 21 46
79117 Freiburg   Email; *mail@monikamusch.de*
Germany.   Website; *http://www.monikamusch.de/*

Contact;
Ralf Netsch,
Waldhäuser Nr. 2,
D-07919 Langenbuch/Thuringen, Tel; 0049 03 6645/2 1328
Germany.   Email; *Netsch99@aol.com*

Peter Noy - Peter Noy has long dedicated himself to making flutes in wood. The finest quality materials, meticulous craftsmanship and intelligent, balanced design are combined to create beautiful instruments, sought after world-wide for their sound.

Contact;
Peter Noy,
1029 NE 69th Street,   Tel; 01 206 729-1903
Seattle, Washington 98115'   Email; *cwpn@mindspring.com*
USA   Website; **http://www.noyflutes.com/**

Contact;
Herbert Paetzold,   Tel; 0049 8342 899 111
Schwabenstrasse 14   Email; *herbert.paetzold@blockfloetenbau-online.info*
D-87640 Ebenhofen,   Website; *www.alte-musik.info/*

Contact;
Luca de Paolis
Piazza Aia di Pile n 9,
67100 L'Aquila,
Italy.

Tel; 0039 862 313103
Email; *ludepa@tiscalinet.it*
Website; *http://www.ldpflautidolci.net/*

Contact;
Peter van der Poel,
Zr. Spinhovenlaan 12,
NL-3981 CS Bunnik,
Holland.

Tel; 0031 030 656 4488
Email; *peter@petervanderpoel.nl*
Website; *http://www.petervanderpoel.nl/index.html*

Martin Praetorius - began his apprenticeship as a woodwind maker with Moeck in 1978. After qualifying he became head of tuning for recorders with interests in development of new instruments, and training of new makers. In 1992 he became a master woodwind maker founded his own workshop, where he makes both baroque and renaissance recorders as well as dulcians and shawms.

Contact;
Martin Praetorius,
Am Amsthof 4,
D-29355, Beedenbostel,
Germany.

Tel; 00 49 5145 93234
Email; *mail@martin-praetorius.de*
Website; *http://www.martin-praetorius.de/*

Contact;
Tom Prescott,
14 Grant Road,
Hanover NH 03755,
USA.

Tel; 001 (603) 643 6442
Email; *recorders@aol.com*
Website; *http://prescottworkshop.com/*

Contact;
Yoav Ran,
5 Benjamin Street,
76244 Rehovot,
Israel.

Tel; 00972 8-9452526
Email; *ran936@bezeqint.net*

Current Active Individual Recorder Makers.

Paul Richardson – originally came from Memphis, Tenn. USA and after finishing his degree in Economics he came to Madrid and studied both lute and recorder.

In 1979, after finishing his studies in the Madrid Royal Conservatory, he founded the Aulos Quartet which has performed throughout North America and Europe. He started making recorders in 1987 after studying with Alec Loretto in Austria.

Contact;
Paul Richardson,
c/- Vaquerias 8-5aD, Tel; 0034 91 4094726
Madrid 28007, Email; *prichard@arrakis.es*
Spain. Website; *http://www.prichard.arrakis.es/*

Contact;
Joachim Rohmer,
Breite Str. 39, Tel; 00 49 5141 217298
D-29 221 Celle, Email; *info@rohmer-recorders.de*
Germany. Website; *http://www.rohmer-recorders.de/*

Bruno Reinhard studied musicology at the University of Strasbourg which at the time offered a diploma in early music, including courses on analysis, notation, and the study of early music treatises. At the same time, he taught recorder lessons in several music schools and gave concerts with several ensembles. In October of 1980 he moved to Provence with 15 orders for his first recorder model, a 17th c. soprano (handfluit) in A 415 that he had designed while still a student. He continued with a hand-fluit (A 415), a baroque alto (A 415) after Stanesby Junior, and a Ganassi alto in G, (A 466 and 440).

Contact;
Bruno Reinhard,
489 Chemin du Bouquier Tel. : +33 04 90 62 39 20
84330 Caromb, Email; *bruno.reinhard@laposte.net*
France. Website *www.flutes-bruno-reinhard.com*

Joanne G. Saunders - was educated at Preshil School where her love of the recorder and woodwork were able to combine. Later, after completing Oboe studies at the Victorian College of the Arts, Joanne persuaded renowned recorder-maker Fred Morgan to train her. Joanne completed a four-year training and set up her own workshop, first in Daylesford, and, after working in Europe for three years, is now living in Melbourne. Joanne specializes in making Baroque Recorders after J.Steenbergen (Amsterdam 18th C). Each instrument is individually hand-crafted and many hours spent 'playing in' and adjusting the voicing to produce a unique tonal characteristic. All instruments are made from selected Honduras Rosewood, European Boxwood, North American Rock Maple and Australian native Mulga woods. Joanne's workshop is currently at the Abbotsford Convent where these beautiful instruments are made.

Contact;
Joanne Saunders,
Abbotsford Convent,
1 St Heliers Street,   Tel; 0061 409 143 942
Abbotsford, Vict. 3067   Email; *jgsrecs@bigpond.net.au*
Australia.   Website; *http://www.abbotsfordconvent.com.au/community/artists/joanne_saunders*

Ella Siekman - Ella Siekman studied the recorder at the Utrecht conservatorium, graduating in 1983. Following this she decided to become a recorder-maker. First she undertook intensive research of authentic historical tools for recorder-building, studying with Sverre Kolberg. Next she studied originals in Vienna, Nuremberg and The Hague. She cooperated with the production of the measurements for the book Dutch Recorders of the 18th Century ... (Acht et al, 1991). She has made recorders professionally since 1989.

Contact;
Ella Siekman,
Dorpsweg 129,
1676 GH Twisk,
Amsterdam,   Tel; 0031 0227 548288
Holland.   Email; *siekmanblokfluitbouw@quicknet.nl*

Contact;
Jaqueline Sorel,
Kazernestraat 96D,   Tel; 0031 703656170
2514 CW Den Haag,   Email; *jacqueline@sorel-recorders.nl*
Holland.   Website; *http://www.sorel-recorders.nl*

Contact;
Martin Wenner,
Aluminiumstrasse 8,   Tel; 00 49 773164085
D 78224 Singen,   Email; *office@wennerfloeten.de*
Germany.   Website; *http://wennerfloeten.de*

Current Active Individual Recorder Makers.

Apologies for any omissions – please contact me for inclusion in a second edition.

References;
1. The Recorder Homepage http://www.recorderhomepage.net
2. Renaissance recorder database http://www.adrianbrown.org/database

Obedience Training for Recorders - *Tim Cranmore*

Current Active Individual Recorder Makers.

Obedience Training for Recorders - *Tim Cranmore*

www.ingramcontent.com/pod-product-compliance
Lightning Source LLC
Chambersburg PA
CBHW081205170426
43197CB00018B/2934